# Grace & Glory

# KAREN DROLLINGER

# Grace & Glory

PROFILES OF FAITH AND COURAGE
IN THE LIVES OF TOP WOMEN ATHLETES

WORD PUBLISHING
Dallas · London · Vancouver · Melbourne

GRACE AND GLORY: PROFILES OF FAITH AND COURAGE IN THE
LIVES OF TOP WOMEN ATHLETES

Unless otherwise indicated, Scripture quotations are from The New American Standard
Bible, © 1960, 1962, 1963, 1968, 1971, 1972, 1973, 1975, 1977 by The Lockman Founda-
tion. Scripture quotations marked NKJV are from the New King James Version, copyright
© 1979, 1980, 1982, Thomas Nelson, Inc., Publisher. Those marked NIV are from the
Holy Bible, New International Version. Copyright © 1973, 1978, International Bible
Society. Used by permission of Zondervan Bible Publishers.

**Library of Congress Cataloging-in-Publication Data**

Drollinger, Karen Rudolph, 1954–
    Grace and glory : profiles of faith and courage in the lives of
top women athletes / Karen Rudolph Drollinger.
        p.    cm.
    ISBN 0-8499-3185-1
    1. Women athletes—Biography.  2. Sports—Religious aspects.
I. Title.
GV697.A1D74    1990
796'.0194'0922—dc20
[B]
                           90-35095
                           CIP

*Printed in the United States of America*

0 1 2 3 4 9    BKC    9 8 7 6 5 4 3 2 1

I'd like to dedicate this book to my mother, *Barbara Rudolph*, and my late father, *Moss*, who as my parents taught me how to be an athlete from a very young age, and to my twin sister, *Sharon*.

To my mother, who always encouraged and never criticized, and who cared about each one of my victories and defeats as though it were her very own.

To my father, who taught me about hard work and discipline in work or play, and who made sure I had the best equipment, insisting I use it consistently and take care of it in order to reach my potential.

To Sharon, my birthmate and teammate, who was always so quick to learn new skills and has always been so self-sacrificing.

Thank you.

# Contents

# Acknowledgments

A special thanks to my husband, Ralph, for dreaming with me when I first suggested this project and then helping me see the possibilities for it.

A great thanks to my children, John, Susan, and young Scott for their patience in seeing me through the creative and writing process.

A deep thanks to Florence Littauer of Christian Leaders and Speakers Seminars and to Barbara Bueler of CLASS for improving my abilities to communicate.

A wholehearted thanks to treasured friends like Roberta, Sandy, Jan, Janet, Cindi, Nancy, Jodie, Kathy, Linda, and so many others who have supported me through this time by their prayers and encouragement.

Much appreciation to Judith Fikse for her loving care of Scott, and to Betsy's Typing Service in Crestline, California, for the transcriptions.

Much appreciation to New Focus, Inc., the Fellowship of Christian Athletes, and Athletes in Action for their interest and research assistance.

> Praise the Lord, all nations; Laud Him, all peoples!
> For His lovingkindness is great toward us,
> And the truth of the Lord is everlasting.
> Praise the Lord!
>
> Psalm 117:1–2

# Introduction

From sorority girls to farmers' daughters, from those with roots in urban slums to those with suburban opportunities, from the well-publicized to the unknown, from wives and mothers to single women, each woman selected for this book has exhibited through her lifestyle a certain grace and glory. There is such a rich diversity of character displayed through each chapter as the athletes share their struggles and relate how Jesus Christ has made a difference in their lives.

Their stories express how women can compete successfully, gaining in grace and confidence as athletes and individuals, and yet retain the strengths of feminine qualities. Like many non-athletic women, they, too, have had to overcome self-image problems, and handle both success and heartache in their lives. Repeatedly, each athlete has emphasized to me the importance of developing her individual talent to the maximum in order to glorify God.

Competitors all, these women have overcome everything from insults to injuries to become champions in their chosen sports. Setting and reaching goals is never easy, but often, they say, the best comfort when undergoing struggles is found in the Bible. For instance, Romans 8:37 says that "We are more than conquerors through him who loved us (NIV)." Conquering here means more than winning a game or match or championship; it means conquering those human tendencies such as quitting, becoming discouraged, criticizing referees, blaming others, being jealous, bragging, showing off, cheating, or putting yourself before the team.

As I have gotten to know each of these women, I've discovered that each one is confident in her Lord and Savior Jesus Christ. I have chosen to highlight their feminine qualities because I fully believe femininity fulfills a woman's godly qualities. Men and women, although equal in their positions before God, were created for different roles. Femininity may not help a female athlete shoot free-throws better, but accepting and fulfilling one's godly image gives her inner confidence to perform to the best of her ability. In other words, femininity is a necessity if women athletes are to be all that God created them to be.

Some of the women in this book have reached that ultimate spot of being number one in their sport. Others have labored unbeknownst to many. Nevertheless, all have a personal story of commitment and faith in God they want to share. May these stories of their lives of grace and glory bring encouragement to all who read them—athlete and sports fan alike.

# Madeline Manning Mims

## 1

## Running the good race

OF ALL THE PEOPLE four-time Olympian Madeline Manning Mims has met during her illustrious track career, no encounter has been more memorable or poignant than that with Yugoslavian half-miler Vera Nikolic. Despite language barriers and racing rivalries, their relationship has come to portray to Madeline a deeper purpose for her athletic competition.

Their rivalry was as intense as any in track and field in the late sixties and early seventies. Madeline was the top-ranked 800-meter runner in the Western hemisphere and Vera was tops in the East. The rivals faced off at a 1967 Europe vs. the Americas meet in Montreal. When Madeline broke into the lead, Vera knocked her off the track and onto the infield. "She was such a fierce competitor," Madeline recalls. "She was a winner at heart and she hated losing. That's one of the reasons she hit me and knocked me off the track. I knew I had a lot left leaning into that curve. That's when she ran up on me as hard as she could and pow! There it all went. I hated it because I was on my way to being the first woman to break two minutes in 800 meters. I was starting to get away from her and I guess she didn't know how else to stop me, so she whacked me."

Startled, Madeline got angry. The adrenaline kicked in like a fill-up at the gas station. "Even after falling, rolling over, getting back up on the track, and struggling to the finish line, I still won in 2:01. So you know I was going to be under that before I fell."

Madeline met Vera again the next year in an 800-meter semifinal heat in the Mexico City Olympics. Again, Madeline was dominating the race when Vera tried a more serious solution. She

1

quit the race after 300 meters, strode out of the stadium, ran to a bridge, and tried to jump off. Her coach caught her before she fell but because of the suicide attempt team officials insisted on returning her to Yugoslavia.

Madeline recalls the incident today, over twenty years later, and the impact it had on her life.

On my way to the stadium for the finals, my teammates told me that Vera was standing by the gate, and I turned around and saw her. She was standing beside guards in front of the women's dormitories while someone upstairs packed up her clothes. Everything in me was saying, "You need to go on, you've got your finals, your coach is waiting on you."

And yet that still small voice was saying, "turn around." When I went over to her, I had never seen anyone so devoid of life. At that point I had just never looked in anybody's eyes and seen that kind of darkness, and it frightened me.

I didn't know what to do or say and finally I just kept calling her name, shaking her. She finally looked up at me but there was no real response. Her arms were down by her side, her face was just pale.

I can't even recall what she was wearing; all I remember is her face.

Vera, approximately the same age as Madeline (twenty) but without her unfettered hope for life, seemed unreachable. Yet Madeline's actions would speak across language barriers.

I was trying to tell her that she was one of the greatest athletes in the world, that she was young, and that she could put it behind her; I tried to encourage her. Finally I said, "Listen, God made you." I began to share my faith and that she was an athlete that God made and that He didn't want her to give up now, that He had not given her that expertise so she could just quit and try to die.

I told her, "Vera, you've got to go back and put all this away from you, get away from it for a while. You've got to find God in your life because you don't have any answers now."

Even though Vera was physically unable to understand Madeline's words spoken in English, she was touched by the message of concern and caring and she began to weep.

"I realized that somehow the Lord had bonded our hearts together. I just took her into my arms and I wept with her, and then I left," Madeline recalls.

Hours later, Madeline won the Olympic gold medal, setting a new American and Olympic record time, and winning by nearly

50 meters. She could hear her mother's voice shouting as she crossed the finish line, but she still couldn't believe she had won. It wasn't until three weeks after the Games that it finally sunk in: she was an Olympic champion.

> I was in a taxicab with my brother, eating an ice cream cone while we were driving down the street. The vision of winning my race came back and I saw myself running and crossing the finish line. I just screamed and threw up my hands. There was ice cream all over the cabbie and he pulled over and asked if I was okay. My brother jokingly said, "Yeah, she just found out she won the gold medal."
>
> I had been a starry-eyed little girl and the youngest on the track team. I was tops in the world at the time, but no one really believed in me. I'm not sure I really believed in myself either. It was like I was there to produce what I had trained so hard for, but I never saw myself as an Olympic gold medalist.

Today, Madeline is the mother of a teenager, college student John Jackson, and a toddler, preschooler Lana Cherelle. She is a traveling speaker and gospel singer now. She has been married to Roderick Mims since December 1978. An earlier brief marriage ended in divorce.

But in 1968 she was a lanky Tennessee State University student capturing an Olympic gold medal just eight years after her idol, Wilma Rudolph, had won three in Rome (more than anyone else in the 1960 Games). Wilma's legacy of three gold medals and a similar history of overcoming a serious childhood illness had always inspired Madeline. Yet growing up in a Cleveland ghetto, it never seemed possible that Madeline could ever attain anything worthwhile, much less Olympic success.

When Madeline was born January 11, 1948, the whole ghetto attitude was, she recalls, "You ain't nuthin', you ain't gonna ever be nuthin', so don't even try."

Drug dealers, prostitutes, and gang members were a reality in her community like doctors, lawyers, and bankers were in other neighborhoods. Mr. Rogers definitely didn't live there.

> Living in the ghetto is a survival-type thing where nobody cares about anybody else. If you can get away with something, you try. But there's a strengthening element, too, because if you can make it through that you can become very strong. For me that happened because of my mother—Queen Saulsberry is her name, and she's just that—a queen—who was a real prayer warrior.

When I was small, I had to survive gangs, prostitution all around, and fighting with knives. It was a terrible situation, but one that made me. I wanted to be somebody and I didn't like what I was seeing. I knew there had to be a better life. You fought for survival, but because of your surroundings you didn't really believe you could be successful in life. But my mother did, and it really helped me to look forward to becoming somebody someday.

That fight for survival began at age three when Madeline contracted a severe case of spinal meningitis. In 1951 such cases often resulted in death, or physical and mental retardation. Doctors gave her mother little hope that she'd survive, much less have a normal childhood. While her mother prayed unswervingly, Madeline gradually regained her health. Nevertheless, Madeline was still sickly and anemic, and painfully shy as a child. But Queen, who worked as a domestic, and Madeline's stepfather, a Baptist minister, believed a good education could vault her from the ghetto. So they enrolled her in a private church-related school. Madeline looks back and describes herself as tall, thin, uncoordinated, dumb, and the ugliest thing in the world. Seems like she might have valued the family dog more, if they had had one.

Now, she says,

When I think back on my childhood, I want to take this message of hope back where I came from and tell those kids that they can make it, too. If I can make it through a broken home, through divorce, through alcoholism in my family, through sickness and death, then they can, too. I tell them that God is on their side. As a Christian athlete I've always tried to portray a loving attitude, a listening ear, and a care and concern about other people. I want to take the gold medal back to the ghetto and let them see it and touch it and build their hope. I want to exhort them to become champions in whatever they endeavor.

Madeline's sentiments emanate from her mother's strong faith in God and her example of tending to the needs of sick and distraught neighbors, of putting on a pot of beans and making cornbread to share with the hungry. Church was an important part of that lifestyle of reaching out to serve others. Though she was an introvert, Madeline says from childhood on she had a desire to love and help people too, and has played that same role. She recalls that other parents in the ghetto would send their kids out to play with her because she would organize activities. "It was free babysitting," she laughs. "We would play house and I'd pretend to feed them and sometimes I would actually take them into my house and feed them."

When Madeline was six, a Sunday school teacher showed a picture of Jesus holding a little black lamb. Madeline asked if Jesus could hold her like that. When the teacher nodded yes and asked if Madeline wanted to invite Him to live in her heart, she closed her eyes and prayed, and pictured herself, like that baby lamb, being held. That wonderful teacher reassured little Madeline that Jesus would always hold her like that. The next Sunday when the pastor asked during the service if she'd accepted Christ, she answered with such a hearty "Yes, sir!" that the entire congregation broke up laughing. "I think she means it," he said. And she did.[1]

Not long afterwards a speaker came to the church preaching a message about "Here am I Lord, send me." Madeline says,

> I didn't know what he was talking about, but at the time I figured he was telling us that God was looking for somebody to go somewhere. I knew I was available, and I wanted to get out of the ghetto. I went back to my little bedroom in the projects and I'll never forget kneeling down at the bed and saying to Jesus, "If all your angels get tied up and busy and all your servants are out and you ain't got nobody to go for you, send me. I'll go."[2]

Though it would be a while before that desire was fulfilled, Madeline got going in other directions. While running in grade-school races, she set a national record in the 50-yard dash with her fluid style and she began receiving attention from track coaches. With additional time and work she tried out for and made a Cleveland track club with a specialty in the 400 meters. Once, the coach sent her to Toronto, Canada, to gain experience in the half-mile and she ended up setting a world indoor record the first time she competed at that distance! At seventeen she made her first national team by winning an Amateur Athletic Union 800-meter title and traveled to compete in Russia, Poland, and West Germany.

Madeline graduated from John Hay High School and was recruited by Ed Temple, the 1960 Olympic women's track coach and head coach at Tennessee State University, Wilma Rudolph's alma

---

1. "The Second Time Around," *Sports Illustrated*, vol. 70, no. 2 (9 January 1989).
2. Ibid.

mater. In an era when female athletes were looked upon as big, tough freaks, TSU took women's track as seriously as most schools would take football. In order to combat criticism, Temple insisted that the women have time to comb their hair and compose themselves before any postrace pictures were taken. He wanted the athletes to be "ladies first and runners second," Madeline says.

In 1960 and 1964 the TSU women provided the United States with a total of eight gold and three silver Olympic medals. In 1968 there would be eight Olympians from TSU competing in Mexico City, including two who represented foreign teams (Costa Rica and Jamaica).

In addition to their daily track practice, the girls worked for their scholarships by sorting letters in the mail room.

In 1968 Madeline became the first American woman to win a gold medal in the 800 meters, considered a long-distance race at the time, although longer distances up to and including the marathon (added in 1984) have subsequently been added. In early Olympiads women were considered incapable of the longer distances after one contestant collapsed following a short-distance race.

Furthermore, many women didn't get involved in athletics in the sixties because of the gender barrier—it was generally considered unfeminine. "It was socially unacceptable then for a woman to be in sports. You were labeled unfairly," Madeline says. "Plus, here was a black person running the 800 meters, which was considered a distance race back then. All the blacks were supposed to be sprinters. I was breaking two rules."

When Madeline approached the dejected Yugoslavian Vera Nikolic in Mexico City perhaps she was breaking another. It was unusual for an athlete to fraternize with the competition, much less a young woman from behind the Iron Curtain, protected by communist authorities.

The next summer Madeline ran in another USA vs. Europe meet in Augsburg, West Germany. She had been the top-ranked half-miler for three years. As she warmed up, she was approached by an unfamiliar man who introduced himself as Vera Nikolic's coach. He told Madeline that Vera was improving but that she wouldn't be running the 800 that day. Madeline's heart was lifted, but she says she was relieved she wouldn't have to race against her rival. The coach continued speaking.

As he did he broke down with tears flooding his eyes. "All these months Vera has been in psychological therapy and she has never talked," the coach said. "But when she finally did break and say something, the first thing that she said was 'Madeline came back and she was on her way to her finals.'"

Madeline recalls,

> When he said that, I knew why I had been born and why God made me an athlete. It was not so much to win gold medals or set world records, but it was to be in the places where He needed me to give encouragement and release the life of Christ in someone else's life.
>
> By that time we were both weeping and I heard someone calling my name across the field. I turned around and it was Vera, running toward me. The first thing she did was grab me and shake me and say, "I found God, I found God!" And I saw this light in her face and from that point we became very good friends.

Madeline would have difficult experiences herself to overcome. One was a failed marriage to a TSU football player with whom she had a son, John. She continued training through the first four months of her pregnancy before she realized she was pregnant. After a 1972 divorce Madeline, now a young single mother with a two-year-old continued competing athletically and working to complete her sociology degree. There were difficulties, but not regarding her ability to come back physically.

"It didn't change my body at all; but it did make me more serious about what I was doing. I wasn't just out there having fun competing anymore. This was something I realized could help me if I had to live single all the rest of my life. I would have a platform that I could use to help me get into other spheres of interest." Her mother, who had moved to Louisiana, helped out from time to time caring for Madeline's son, so Madeline could continue to pursue her degree and another gold medal.

In 1972, the Olympic Games were hosted by the city of Munich, West Germany. Many Americans today remember that Olympiad as being both joyful—it was the year gymnast Olga Korbut captivated worldwide audiences and swimmer Mark Spitz won seven gold medals—and yet tragic. It is impossible to think about the Munich Olympics without remembering the young Israeli athletes taken hostage and killed by terrorists. It was also a controversy-filled Olympiad. The American men's basketball team lost to the Russians on a referee's controversial decision and two American sprinters were told incorrect starting times and failed to show up in time for their events. Madeline herself, overjoyed to be on her second Olympic squad and elected a team captain, was not to escape controversy.

In prerace instructions, judges had indicated the wrong finish line for the 800 meters, and Madeline, the defending gold medalist, coasted after thinking she would qualify easily. "I remember what I did wrong: I was always taught to run past the finish line twenty to thirty yards before stopping and I didn't do that. I slowed down and started walking off the track." But out of the corner of her eye she could see a competitor lunging for the correct finish line and instinctively, she responded, at once horrified and disbelieving.

"It took the officials fifteen minutes to decide that I missed the finals by 2 centimeters, and I was crushed," Madeline says, describing how she was comforted in the waiting room by Vera Nikolic. "She sat very quietly beside me and waited. When they came in with the news she just put her arm around me and said, 'That's all right. You've got plenty of years. You're still young and you've got God on your side.' It was like the Lord used her to minister to me." After comforting others with the comfort with which God has comforted her, that day Madeline needed Vera's reminder of His constant caring.

But the frustration welled up like an slumbering volcano. That night, Madeline remembers sitting in one of the Olympic Village restaurants talking with her coach when it suddenly overwhelmed her like a malevolent thunderstorm. She tried to hurl a soft drink bottle through a plate-glass window but the coach's wife caught her arm. Madeline tossed the bottle down and ran screaming down a flight of stairs, and locked herself in the bathroom. "I just screamed and banged on the doors and all the frustration of the entire year was coming out then—the divorce and all the work I'd put in. There are some times in your life that you go through that are so intense, but they definitely make you build your faith."

In Munich the athletes' hope and joy expressed in the memorable opening ceremonies was shattered by the murder in the Olympic compound of eight Israeli athletes by a Palestinian terrorist group, Black September. Madeline says that it interrupted the harmony of the world's youth who were trying to compete and live together peacefully.

Usually when you are in the Olympic Village you are protected from what is going on in the outside world. It's an athlete's utopia and you don't even care about what's going on elsewhere. You are just enjoying that moment and meeting and talking to different people that you've seen and heard on television and read about in magazines. The terrorists were trying to make their point to the world and they used something so innocent as athletes and they brought in this violence and hatred and anger and killed innocent people.

The Games continued in somber remembrance and Madeline had another opportunity to win a medal in the 4-X-400-meter relay.

Despite a severely pulled muscle, she ran gamely and the Americans finished with a silver medal. "I did my best and ran one of the hardest races of my life because it really hurt to run, but I was not going to let my team or my country down."

Following the disappointments of 1972, Madeline retired from track and began ministering, speaking boldly in the media about her faith, and singing and sharing in prisons with former Cleveland Brown tight-end-turned-evangelist Bill Glass. In 1975 she was elected to the Track and Field Hall of Fame. Yet the next year Madeline, still feeling competitive, decided her retirement had been premature and returned to seek a berth in the 1976 Games in Montreal. At twenty-eight, her age was considered a handicap, but she felt stronger than ever. That year she became the first American woman to break two minutes in the 800 meters (1:59.8), and she was selected the outstanding female athlete at the Olympic Trials. Once more, Olympic glory seemed virtually assured, but once more there was tragedy. And with it, remarkably, there was another opportunity to tell the world about her faith in Christ.

In the semifinals, Madeline ran lethargically, practically sleepwalking through her heat and missing the cut, finishing last with a time of 2:07.

I've tried to figure it out—did I freak out, did I get scared, was there too much pressure (but I'd always had that type of pressure so I was used to it)—but the flow just wouldn't come out. I was watching television from the back of the pack; that's what you call it when you're in the back and there's nothing you can do about it except watch everybody run away from you. I was frustrated when I came through that finish line and I couldn't figure out what went wrong. When I walked out of the stadium through the tunnel I was mobbed by the news media with their cameras, microphones, tape recorders, pencils and notebooks, and everybody was talking at the same time.

I'll never forget what this one guy asked. I was crying and he said, "I know you're hurting and I'm sorry to put you under this type of pressure, but we need an answer. You've been telling everybody all over the world, behind the Iron Curtain and here in America and in Montreal while you've been here, that you've been running for Jesus. Well, what we want to know is, are you going to still run for Jesus or are you going to try something else?"

It shocked me that he would even ask a question like that, but I understood where he was coming from because when you stand up for Jesus sometimes people don't understand.

And I finally just said, "You know what—at five o'clock in the morning when I was running in the hail and snow and the rain and it was below zero, you guys weren't there, but Jesus was. And when I had to work an eight-hour job and come back and take care of a kid and then go out three or four more hours to train, until I was totally fatigued—day after day, week after week, and month after month, and on into years—there was no one there but Jesus in my life to keep motivating me and inspiring me and driving me.

"So my answer is that as long as I live, whether it be on that track or whether I'm running in another of life's arenas, I'll always run for Jesus." When that response went worldwide I realized the race was not on the track, it was right there in front of the whole world.

Two weeks after the 1976 Olympics, Madeline redeemed her poor outing and set a new American record at College Park, Maryland, in 1:57.9 (which held until 1983, when it was broken by Mary Decker). She retired again but returned to the track in 1978 after moving to Tulsa and becoming engaged to Roderick Mims.

When I got to Tulsa, the Lord began to deal with my heart about running again and I said, "No, I don't wanna." I knew He wasn't just talking about running around the block, you know. I knew He was talking about going for the gold and I was afraid. But Rod, my fiancé, encouraged me to do whatever God told me to do because I wouldn't be happy otherwise. I was hoping Rod would get me out of it, but he locked me into it.

Rod and Madeline were married December 23, 1978. Her new name, Madeline Manning Mims, rolls euphonically off the tongue, reminding one of the regal bearing with which she carries herself. After their marriage, she worked on a graduate degree at Oral Roberts University and continued to raise John.

In 1980 Madeline qualified for her fourth Olympics, winning the 800 by 15 meters in a trials record of 1:58.3, her best time since returning to the track.

I attribute all my comebacks to the Lord. I didn't really believe in me; in fact I questioned Him. I said, "Are you sure?" When He said yes, then I stepped out by faith and kind of tried it again and I found that I did have something left. That's basically when He spoke to my heart and said, "Mad, you got more left and you can't give up until you've given it all out." And true enough, my very last years in '80 and '81 were my best running years ever.

Those years were satisfying personally in other ways.

The 1980 Olympic Trials were probably the highlight because I was using my running as an opportunity to share the love of God with my teammates and the world. I could easily have quit when the boycott was announced; perhaps there was no use in continuing to run. But I looked around and saw my teammates needed someone to take some leadership. I wanted to exhort and uplift and edify the team. So I said, "We're not called to just be in the Olympic games. We are athletes who have worked to produce and we'll have other opportunities to compete in other countries."

Despite much controversy about the boycott, the decision stood, and President Jimmy Carter and the United States Olympic Committee honored the athletes in late July at the White House. Madeline, elected a captain of the women's track team for a third time, says she encouraged everyone to support and not criticize that decision, and display unity and a challenging "never give up attitude" for a future generation of athletes who *would* be able to compete in the Olympics.

In the athletic arena there's a lot of pressure and fear, and there are opportunities to touch someone's life when they are vulnerable. I took being captain as more than an honorary position; I took it as an opportunity to serve, from giving rubdowns to talking with someone at 2:00 in the morning to finding someone's sweats. I'd pray with people and try to keep their spirits up. The Lord just placed me in a position to be a spiritual leader as well as a team captain.

Madeline was also selected, along with four-time Olympic pentathlete Bob Nieman, to give the athletes' response to President Jimmy Carter's address to the assemblage. Look to the future, support upcoming young athletes, unite in America as a family, increase the financial support to amateur athletics, she implored. And she asked for God's blessing to come forth.

"I truly believe that came to pass in 1984 in Los Angeles," she says. "The most magnificent thing I've seen in my life was to watch the Los Angeles games come together and to see the beauty of this nation come together as a family, uniting as one, encouraging and motivating. It was just phenomenal."

Not long after she completed her last race in December of 1981 in Venezuela, she incorporated Madeline Manning Mims Ministries (renamed Friends Fellowship in 1987), with a commission to reach young people and exhort them with a message of hope, and to share the gospel with women in prison.

In prisons, I get down to the nitty-gritty and tell them exactly where I came from. I put myself where they are and let them know that I easily could be where they are with the situation I came out of, but that I chose to follow Jesus and in so choosing it brought me success. I say, "I came here to give you the best I've got and that's Jesus."

It doesn't matter to me if someone says I sang real nice or that was a beautiful presentation or a nice speech or that's neat that you're an Olympian. That doesn't amount to a hill of beans for me if I don't see a heart changed. I've wasted their time and God's. But when I actually see a life change and be born again then that makes my time and their time very much redeemed. I want to leave this world knowing that someone's life was changed because I shared with them a message of hope: that they can believe once again that God can start working in their life.

In the prisons when I speak, it's a growing experience for me as well as for those listening. With the women, I feel that but for the grace of God I could be there. I've been through some pretty rough things in my life and I've come close to going off the deep end and having that happen to me. I put myself in their place and try to feel what they're feeling.

The greatest compassion that you can ever have is to be able to cry when someone else is crying, when you yourself might be happy; or to rejoice when somebody else is rejoicing, even though you might be sad. I'm learning through these ladies to love unconditionally, without knowing faults or placing values, by just being able to give all I can.

That all comes from my realizing what God has done in my life. If God can deal with me he can deal with anybody. I am a strong-willed woman who loves winning—I'm not too good of a loser. But I've learned to use all of the valleys as a stepping stone to move up higher. I never use those valleys to hold myself down, but always to evaluate what I did wrong and then use that to help somebody else. Wherever I'm speaking I want to be able to share the life-changing process that Christ has done within me.

After nine years of marriage to Rod, Lana Cherelle was born and Madeline, nearly forty by now, felt like she was starting anew. "When you're young you never know what you're going to be doing at forty and what's going to be happening at this time in life. With my little baby daughter I feel like I've been given some years back to enjoy," she says. She feels more settled and at peace, and more patient in training this child than she might have been at a younger age, she says. And her son, John, is blossoming into manhood and making decisions on his own. Madeline encourages him to be obedient to God, not because she or Rod say to, but because God is with him and can help him make crucial decisions. "It's the hardest thing to let go of those strings and not latch onto him. The Lord's only let me be with him for a little while. My family is so important to me, yet I also want to minister to hurting people."

The fulfillment of being a wife and mother gives me balance. I can come home after ministering and find my refuge and strength and peace and love and joy, and I can be Madeline. People expect a lot from you, they take a lot of strength from you, and you have to give as much as possible until you give it all out. Then I can come home and be refilled again with the love of my husband. He's neat and he spoils me. I can be all those things I can't be out there. At home, I can pout and I can cry. There I find strength and encouragement. And I realize I couldn't be doing what I am without him. There's no way I could give like that without his completing that part of me that I need.

Home is also the training ground where I learn how to give, how to be patient, how to forgive and be forgiven.

Madeline's favorite verse for signing autographs typifies her focus: "For I am confident of this very thing, that He who began a good work in you will perfect it until the day of Christ Jesus" (Philippians 1:6).

# 2 Margo Oberg

## Changing tides

"HEY, MAN, THE LADY CAN SURF!" exclaimed the Hawaiian boy to his friends surfing on the western shore of Kauai. His comment was not the first such observation about the impressive seven-time world champion surfer Margo Oberg. Others have expressed similar amazement over the past twenty-five years.

Breaking surfing etiquette that day, the youngster had repeatedly cut in on Margo's ride. Generally, the first surfer up close to the whitewater (where the best ride is) receives priority. Additional riders cause the wave to break, and ruin a good ride.

Those boys weren't into the latest surfboards or surfing magazines, or they would have known that Margo is a surfing legend with scores of titles, famous from Australia to North Africa. The kids were only intent on having a good time.

In surfing it's survival of the fittest. The boys might as well have been a bunch of "show-me" Missourians. Pros get more waves in surfing hierarchy—but so do big 200-pound locals. A slender, unintimidating woman like Margo could get boxed out if she weren't aggressive.

"One guy kept cutting in front. I was trying to be real patient, but I was getting a little frustrated," she recalls. "But one time he was paddling back out while I was surfing, so it was like I was on stage and he could see me the whole way. Then I could hear him say to his buddies with kind of the local dialect, 'Hey, the lady can surf!' From then on out, he gave me waves."

Swells pushed by storms off the coast of northeast Russia travel twenty-five hundred miles before smacking the Hawaiian coral reef and crashing on shore, creating some of the best waves

14

on earth. With its beautiful azure-colored warm water and impressive breakers, Hawaii is a surfer's paradise.

Margo and Steve Oberg moved to Kauai, the northernmost isle, known as the Garden Island, shortly after their March 1972 wedding. He was twenty-one; she was only eighteen and already a hot-shot surfer.

Indeed, her picture first graced the pages of *Surfer Magazine* when she was only eleven. At the same time, she had write-ups in the *San Diego Union* and the *La Jolla Light*. Then, she was a ninety-eight-pound youngster in pigtails winning a four-foot trophy nearly her own height; today, she's a thirty-six-year-old mother of two (Shane, born in 1982, and Jason, born in 1987) who collects surfboards (she has over twenty) like some people collect coffee cups. She's also a professional instructor with her own surfing school, at the Kiahuna Plantation Resort at Poipu Beach on Kauai's south shore.

Yet with all her success, Margo is not hung up on being a "surf star." She and her husband Steve, a Certified Public Accountant, live a simple life, centered around their main interests: surfing, their family—and, most importantly, their faith in God. Sunday mornings find the Obergs worshiping at the nearby Kalaheo Missionary Church.

Watch a surfing contest on local Saturday night TV and Margo might be competing. Or check out the new Sunset Beach junior line of clothing for Catalina Sportswear, and you'll find she's endorsed it. If you pick up a brochure for surfing lessons on Kauai, chances are she's involved. It sounds so glamorous, but Margo takes it all in stride. Changing diapers and meeting the demands of a family have built her character, she realizes, and have helped her make the transition from superstar to servant, from maverick to mom.

Her girlfriends recognize that she's unique; that God has gifted the 5-foot-5-inch, blue-eyed blonde with a special ability to surf and with a flexible, supportive husband in Steve.

"They'll even tease me—like they'll give me a birthday card with ballerinas on the front and one real funny-looking ballerina will be wearing a fluorescent costume. That one's supposed to be me. They want me to know that I'm special and I'm different, and that they accept that," she says today.

Or I'll be sitting on the floor at a Bible study stretching my legs with a friend of mine who rides boogie boards [smaller, rubbery foam boards that are ridden lying down] and we'll start talking about the waves. Everyone else will start yawning as though we're boring them, but they really accept the novelty of my surfing. My Christian friends are basically secure in themselves and optimistic, with a hope and a vision for their lives.

I feel really loved and accepted within that circle. I never feel like I have to apologize for who I am or what I'm doing. I'd probably ride my mountain bike for miles and miles if I didn't have surfing because I've grown up being used to a lot of exercise.

It's like they see that "God's given Margo this gift to surf and because she is different, she has opportunities to witness to people and help people." I have a real hard time around negative people because I am always trying to cheer them up and make them laugh and see that life's okay.

That's why I think I really like kids. They have such potential. And I let others know I'm happy with being Mom for my own kids when they might think I miss being Margo-the-surf-star.

Margo, the youngest of three children in the Godfrey family, grew up at La Jolla Shores north of San Diego near the Scripps pier (by the renowned Scripps Oceanographic Institute). Her parents, she says, allowed her and her brother Ty and sister Emilie a lot of individual freedom and the beach was a handy babysitter. "Ever since I was five we walked across the street and played in the sand," she recalls.

Margo's father, a former United States Naval Academy letterman (tennis, wrestling), wanted his kids to share his love for sports, but when Ty (four years older than Margo) showed only casual interest, Mr. Godfrey started playing catch with little Margo. From that time, at the age of two, she was Daddy's little girl. Those letters on his award sweater looked pretty impressive, she says. He'd take her fishing and out to play. Soon she wanted to be like her athletic father and that meant taking up his favorite sport: tennis.

She picked up the sport quickly and eventually won a San Diego tournament for kids ten and under. Emilie, a single year older, won the twelve-and-under bracket. And with her father's encouragement, it looked like tennis would be Margo's sport. But Margo hesitated. She was more interested in the beach part of the La Jolla Beach and Tennis Club where they practiced—specifically, the *surf* part of it. She says,

I didn't like the atmosphere of tennis at all. There were people on the sidelines, it was too structured, and everybody got so worked up by it all. I kept looking at the ocean all the time.

One thing that motivated me when I started was just a love for surfing. I liked the isolation, the seclusion—even today I just forget about all the things I have to deal with on land. It's just "Hi, Lord," and I talk to the Lord the whole time I'm out there; thanking Him for the nice day and the beauty. I feel close to God. It's a time for me to sort through the daily things and decide what I am going to make the kids for dinner. While I search through my daily responsibilities then, I also find quiet time to spend with the Lord.

Oh, well. So she traded in sets of tennis for sets of waves. No matter.

Because of its location, the Godfreys' La Jolla home gradually became a storage center for high schoolers' surfboards. "Kids just knocked on the door and said, 'Hi,' and asked if they could store their surfboards in my back yard so they could ride their bikes down from the high school after classes." Margo would hang out on a cement wall along the beach and study the surfers' form and styles.

One such surfer guy was her friend Mitch. He'd pull up in the summer with a trailer and rent rubber rafts and beach equipment. Margo and Mitch would over-inflate the rubber rafts to make them real hard, take them out and stand and ride them in. Before long Mitch took Margo out on a long surfboard and pushed her into a couple of waves so that she could get a feel for it. One time and she was hooked.

"I stood up and rode it all the way in," she reminisces fondly. Waves playfully tickling her toes, slipping effortlessly through the water, paddling forcefully enough to catch waves, sun, and wind— she loved the endless challenge.

"It's a real fitness sport since it takes nearly every muscle in your body. You have to develop good wave judgment because the waves shift around and are all different. You've got to have timing and you've got to bend or twist according to the wave. You're squinting from the glare of the sun and the wind is blowing in your face."

Enthralled, at ten she asked her parents for a surfboard. After a winter of borrowing the high schoolers' stored boards, surfing at 5:30 for an hour before school, then showering and leaving for her elementary school, her parents were impressed and gave in. A surfboard was hers to choose. Her first one cost maybe thirty-five dollars. "I remember driving home from the surf shop in the back of the station wagon totally ecstatic," says Margo. She recalls, gleefully hugging that piece of figerglass the way some girls hug their Barbie dolls.

"I practiced constantly so I could gain respect and seniority, so that I could establish myself within a crowd, so that guys wouldn't drop in on me on a wave because they would know I could surf. In surfing, it's man against nature; it's conquering big waves and meeting sharks."

Margo has had her share of both in her career.

Not long after the movie *Jaws* came out in the early seventies, Margo found herself on Kauai surfing with two men a quarter mile out to sea. She had broken her vow not to see that movie because horror movies had scared her ever since she was small. About a week after viewing it, she spotted a big shark swimming through a transparent swell and she was terrified. "I mean, I knew he had his food because he was after this fish swimming in the swell, but I just panicked. I turned to ride the wave in on my belly, but the wave smashed me and I wiped out."

Separated from her board (leashes hadn't yet become popular) in the churning water, all she could hear was the dreaded theme song from *Jaws*. She did her best eggbeater imitation trying to escape. "I was so panicked I was nearly running on top of the water. I've never swum that fast and I screamed at my friend Ralph. I was hysterical, and he came over and gave me his board and told me to lie down on his board while he swam in. He was a scuba diver familiar with sharks and he cautioned me not to panic, but just to surf on in."

Margo can share many stories about the dangers of surfing in Hawaii. Weather and submerged reefs are two. Today, top pros like Tom Carroll wear helmets similar to bicycle helmets for protection. The head gear keeps a surfer's eardrums from being ruptured when forced under a monstrous wave and protects the head from being gashed on the coral. The helmets are optional, the way motorcycle helmets are in some states. And weather is always a factor.

You paddle out on a certain size board because the waves are a certain size. The bigger the wave the more flotation you need because you need to paddle down the wave. But in Hawaii the storms come up real quick; one set of waves will be eight feet, the next three nine feet, then suddenly they're ten feet and the whole horizon starts picking up with the storm rolling in. You keep being forced further out to sea and the next thing you know the waves are simply too big to catch.

Then it's survival: how do I get back to the beach without drowning? Your board's like a little potato chip. If you had a big board, you might be able to paddle into the thing and stand up and ride it in. But if your board's too small, you feel like one of those little styrofoam containers from the market. You can't even paddle it and the wave just races by you. You're like a little cork bobbing in the water. You can only hope to catch a medium-sized wave and let it drag you to the beach in the whitewater. You basically wash up on the beach.

With experiences like that, surfing was never dull. Ride a board but don't be bored. Margo loved it.

"There are a thousand different things going on—you wonder if you're going to break your board or your body, or if you're going to get dragged over the reef," she says.

And where she grew up in California there was the frigid Alaska Current to contend with. Wetsuits didn't become popular until later, and the chilly waters proved painfully cold. "It was cold, and my hands and feet were numb just like being in the snow. My feet would be totally numb as I walked across the parking lot those mornings and gradually they would thaw out."

By the time Margo finishes her thought the number of variables has grown by tens of thousands. "The whole time you're surfing there's a million different variables, plus the fear factor." Some sport, you say—just right for crazy Californians. Aah, yes; the fear factor.

Below the wave it looks like a little mini-tornado, and you spin around and then usually come up. But sometimes there's so much pressure that you grope for the top and there's no way up.

When I was sixteen I was held under so long that I went from what I'd been taught—relax and don't panic—to full-on panic and thinking I was swimming toward the top when actually I was heading toward the bottom. Then I just lay there, delirious, almost in a state of total relaxation, almost trancelike.

It was so unbelievable. I was probably starting to black out a little bit because I'd been under about two minutes. It just all happened so fast. I had my eyes open and I could see all these little fish swim by and I can remember thinking of that song by the Beatles called "Octopus's Garden." I was just lying there, dreaming and thinking my life was over and how sad my mom would be and how everybody would hear on the radio that Margo had died surfing.

Slowly I kept floating up to the top and I kept having this feeling like this Supreme Being or this Force was rescuing me, even though I never went to church or had deep thoughts about God. I kept having this feeling that God was helping me up. When I came to the surface I was really excited to be alive. Then after that when anybody would mention God, or peace, or meditation, I was really tuned in.

Thinking those things were the answer to her spiritual needs, Margo investigated Eastern philosophies and mysticism, and even began reading the Bible. Like many in the late sixties, Margo was influenced by that era's spiritual and social activism. It seemed like every popular rock group had its Indian guru; the Reverend Martin Luther King was leading racial boycotts; the "Jesus movement" swelled; there were love-ins and peace marches—a cause for everybody and everybody for a cause. While Margo pondered inward things and asked questions, there were other events taking place in her life.

At age sixteen, Margo flew to Puerto Rico and won her first world title, along with *Surfer Magazine*'s Number One ranking for women in 1968 and 1969.

As a child, I had sort of a self-imposed isolation in training because I really wanted to win. I wanted to be a champion. My girlfriends might suggest shopping at the mall for three hours, and I would go but I'd be thinking about all the good waves I was missing. The best surfers were usually the guys, so I think I had a steady boyfriend since the seventh grade. I would always end up being with my boyfriend surfing.

I think I got all the recognition early for being a girl who just put it all together. All the guys would go, "that person can surf!" I got their stamp of approval, like "All right, this girl is totally certified, totally accepted, and she really knows how to surf."

There were other girls before me in competition, but as far as being innovative in my whole style, I was a pioneer. Guys were telling me they didn't want to surf against me in contests; that I was the first girl they had seen surf like that. I was a little more slender in my body build and people thought I surfed very femininely or daintily—not dainty, but with just a real feminine gracefulness. When I surf I try to be harmonious with the wave and be graceful and carry off a certain feeling.

The surfing movement, popularized by the Beach Boys' music and the surf movies of the mid sixties with Gidget and the gang, was consolidated even more with publicity through *Surfer Magazine*. Margo reminisces about the fun of surfers pulling up in their vans and station wagons and camping out or all staying in a favorite beach hotel and hanging out together. They'd surf to the max, then gather around a campfire afterward swapping surf stories.

It was almost like the old tribal sort of stuff in a way—very primitive. Most of the history was word-of-mouth. It wasn't like tennis or basketball where you would have documented statistics and legends. When *Surfer Magazine* came out it got a little more unified. I was only ten when I started so I'd sit and watch everybody celebrating.

To me, this group of people were such interesting characters— funny and with great personalities and I was impressed by all their surfing tricks. I liked their sense of adventure, mystique, and exploring. They'd talk about hopping in the car and driving as far down in Mexico as they could and finding this perfect wave and how scary it was. When the contests were amateur, it was more like just having fun. You might get a trophy and a little write-up in the paper or something, but it just wasn't the way everybody made their living.

As the teenage champion warmed herself around the campfires, she'd listen to her male surfing buddies tell dirty jokes and discuss their sexual desires and disrespect for the women who'd give in to their advances. She didn't know how to relate to this, so she'd ask close friends like Mike Doyle, Corky Carroll, and Skip Frye (who all influenced her surfing style, training habits, and competitive desires) what they thought. Their advice: keep it cool, keep a clean reputation, and don't mess around with anyone. She says they taught her how to deal with the public and not to be hung up on herself.

Margo reflects on how things changed when surfing became a professional sport.

When surfing went pro in 1975 it was way more intense. Instead of going to a contest to share and party and enjoy surfing, everybody became separate individuals. They'd get Walkmans and listen to their "psych-out tapes." They'd get their special protein powder and their psychic coach and have their little contest strategies, and the TV cameras would roll over to the winner.

Maybe it wasn't so much money as just the era and changes in the tide. The sixties were so weird—like the love-ins, everybody dropping out and wearing blue jeans and sitting on the beach. It's hard to even define it, but people weren't very materialistic. They were trying not to climb over other people's heads while they were climbing the ladder to success. The creed of the surfing world was to be cool and aloof and self-righteous. "Let's all hang out and not work too hard." Surfers are pioneers in the sense of getting back to nature and leading a simple lifestyle—the idea of Man versus Nature.

Then the pendulum swung the other way, from looking like a total slob and not wanting a job to guys putting gel in their hair and wearing little earrings and even wearing eyeliner and all the Day-Glo fashion clothes. At some of the trade shows I work these guys are as athletic and macho as anybody but too concerned with their image

and how fashionable they are. It's become very materialistic. Sponsor-
ships, being on a certain surf team, how much money is paid to
individuals—it's like people's identities have become wrapped up in
how much money they make, how much sponsorship they get, what
their ranking is, where they're traveling and competing.

Whenever you are going to accumulate material things you are
going to try to put a little fence around them. You are going to try to
protect the materialism. It's like back to the animal kingdom: collect a
few acorns, hide them in your tree; and the dog gets all his bones and
hides them in the ground.

While the tides were changing in the surfing world, they were
also changing in Margo's personal realm. She had met Steve while
he was working for a surfing-related business in Encinitas, California. Steve had come to know the Lord after living in a primitive
tree house on a Hawaiian beach and reading through the Book of
John during his own spiritual odyssey. He'd surf by daylight and
search the Scriptures for meaning by candlelight until he accepted
Jesus Christ as his personal Savior. Steve returned to the mainland
after that seemingly carefree summer intent on growing in his
faith. After a while he began leading songs and worship time at
his church. Steve and Margo were good friends because Margo was
then dating his roommate. But when the pair broke up, Steve
began taking her to Bible studies with other surfer friends, and
within two weeks had asked her to marry him. Margo says she felt
like it was God's divine plan and a year out of high school, she got
married.

Margo and Steve avoided the turmoil of competitive surfing by
moving to Kauai and dropping out for five years, she says. They
searched for perfect, uncrowded waves and she "just learned to be
a nobody." She says she spent those years, "cruising around the
island with Steve," but in reality, they were important to developing a good solid foundation for their marriage.

Margo worked at the beautiful Kiahuna Plantation Resort
as beach services manager and gave surfing lessons, while Steve
worked in accounting. In 1975 when the International Professional
Surfing circuit started, Steve and Margo got involved.

Margo captured world pro titles in 1975, 1976, 1977, and was
rated number one worldwide for most of 1978. She took a year
off to build their new home with Steve, and she did guest com-
mentating for ABC-TV's "Wide World of Sports." Then she
came back to win world titles again in 1980 and 1981 before
Shane's birth in 1982. She was twenty-eight and already had

appeared in cameo roles in eight movies, plus numerous TV commercials and print ads. Additional television appearances included NBC's "Sportsworld," CBS's "Sports Spectacular" and programs like "Challenge of the Sexes" and "Women Superstars" competitions. The "American Sportsman" had flown the Obergs to North Africa so she could join former pro football player Russ Francis in searching for the perfect wave. She even taped an episode for the hit TV show "Magnum P.I.," with Tom Selleck. But the Big G's—Glitz and Glamour—were about to give way to the Big B's—Baby's Bottom, Baby's Bottle, and Baby's Bedtime. Margo describes those times.

> When we first got married, I basically had a career. I was a surfing champion and Steve was my coach. We traveled all over the world, I made most of the money, and he was very supportive of what I was doing. We were involved in our church with an evangelistic youth ministry, so I was in hog heaven and just having a great time.
>
> We were fine until we had kids.

Margo speaks today as though she has been tempered by sacrifice, faithfulness, and dedication—and knows that gaining those qualities exacts a sometimes painful, but invaluable, price.

"It was tough adjusting from being number one in the world, traveling to exotic places and competing really hard, to changing diapers and doing laundry, but those years built my character," she says, recalling the time when Tide and Surf became her steady friends in the laundry room, not at the beach.

> Yet I wouldn't trade that time for anything. When I would go out later and surf and compete I could really appreciate surfing a lot more. Surfing is a young people's sport, and you're the fittest you're going to be when you're eighteen to twenty years old.
>
> Some people, all they do is surf and eat health foods and lie down and take a nap. Sometimes before a contest I'd wish I was in better shape physically or a little more this or that, but I'd counter that by using better strategies.

As Margo matured regarding raising a child, she also came to understand the importance of solid families in God's perfect will.

> I can see Paul's wisdom in saying women be submissive and supportive of your husbands and husbands love your wives like Christ loved the church. We've both had to learn to balance it all, and we still go through that process even now. We're certainly equal before

God in our worth, but Steve and I have differing functions. Our roles are equally important in God's eyes, but different: Steve is to be the spiritual leader of our family and my role is to help raise up godly children.

My old nature might lean toward being a women's libber—you know, "Nobody's going to tell *me* what to do." The woman stays home with the kids and the guy makes all the money and gets all the prestige. I can see where women might want to say, "I worked my way through school, I got an education, I can go surfing or do sports just as well as the guys. I can be just as important, so I deserve equal pay and equal rights and equal freedom, and I deserve the corresponding respect." But my greatest satisfaction comes from taking care of my family.

After having children, everything became a mega-effort because I had increased responsibilities. It's just physically exhausting. So I knew for myself that I probably wouldn't be traveling all over the world again and be on the road ten months a year when I had my first child.

I just felt like I was supposed to hold Shane, feed him, read him a story—I just kind of thought I was supposed to do everything.

There was a real sadness in letting go of the past—and seemingly my youth—like when I turned thirty. I realized I'm not a kid anymore. I'm not going to just think about me. (Because Steve and I had a pretty independent thing where we could surf together and do whatever we wanted.)

But I loved that baby so much I really didn't want to be anywhere else. I would sit back and be nursing my baby, and I wouldn't want to be traveling. I didn't want to compete. I didn't want to go anywhere because I loved this little one so much. There was just a combination between us, a bonding. I'd think, "What a miracle. What a blessing. God gave me this perfect son and he's so cute."

Then another day I'd be walking with the stroller and the baby, and the waves would be six feet and all my friends would be surfing. And at the very beginning I wasn't into having a babysitter at all. I was nursing Shane every day so I was really tied down. And then I'd start feeling sorry for myself.

But it was just a little bit of a change of season, a change of tide.

At the same time Steve enrolled at the University of Hawaii, commuting to Honolulu to obtain his accounting degree. Though it was a difficult transition, Steve was studying to make them happier in the long run. He told Margo he'd provide the income and that her surfing wouldn't support the family forever. Realistically, she knew that to be true; nevertheless, it hit like Arctic ice water.

He was kind of almost rubbing it in, like, "Not that you're a has-been, but. . . . Hey, dear, you were a star and made some money, but now you're a mom and you're not going to be making a lot of money." We really had to juggle our roles for a while so that he could become the breadwinner, or if I did have the opportunity to enter a contest, for him to again be the support person.

During that transition period there was a time of letting go of my competitiveness. I could see where there was an era of achievement, achievement, achievement; there was a time when surfing was real important. But then it was time for kids and family life. I didn't want people to see me as a surf star, an achiever, somebody above them. I wanted everybody to see me neutral. Even today I'll meet somebody and they'll be real impressed that I was a world-champion surfer and want to know all about the biggest wave I ever rode and stuff like that.

But I needed my friends to encourage me—even though my achievements may have made me seem like Supergirl—because I had all the same problems they did in being a mom. It just brought out all the emotions inside me.

I really didn't circulate in the surf crowd at that time because I thought that I was supposed to be a housewife. And every verse in the Bible can seem to pin you to that—that the woman should do the house, be submissive, and be the mother, and not disrupt your family by pursuing a career outside the home.

While Margo treasured her surfing memories, she realized the importance of being a mother, and gradually feelings of satisfaction began to replace the despondency she'd been feeling.

At first I just gave up. I thought "When you're a mom, you're a mom and all you do is take care of kids." That was my priority—when you have a child you take care of them first. I still feel that's true. Just stay home and take care of your kids and don't do your career and don't be in the limelight.

Before, if the waves were big I would feel guilty about leaving the baby with a babysitter just so I could go surfing. Instead of telling myself, "You've been home with the kids all day and you're feeling a little tense, go surfing for an hour," I'd judge myself harshly with unreal expectations. I needed a release. So now I say it's okay and give myself permission to surf when I need to. And part of it was, the youngest, Jason, was getting a little older, and when I'd take him to the sitter he would just run and play with the other two- and three-year-olds. And I knew he would have fun and wouldn't miss me for an hour or two while I went surfing.

There was a lot of happiness in staying home, but there was a lot of confusion too because I had so much creative energy. Surfing is my creative outlet—like someone else singing a song or playing a piano or painting a picture. Whether anyone else sees your painting or not, or whether or not your song makes the top ten and a million dollars you're going to get your artistic thrill out of it. It's the same with me and surfing. It's my creativeness and my artisticness. Whether or not I win a contest or I'm a star because of it, I just love doing it anyway.

Shane was only three months old when Margo competed in the 1982 Sunkist World Cup and placed second. "I nursed him, swam out on my heat, came in and nursed more. I'd paddle lopsided because I'd fed him too much on one side. My girlfriend who was watching him was letting him chomp on her fingers trying to pacify him until I could come in. I got second and I didn't even expect that," Margo recalls. The next year, Margo won the 1983 World Cup.

"But it seemed like the kids came first and that took everything. And then there was my work at the resort. I tried to surf when I could, but I was always tired and never seemed to get enough rest. And I wasn't feeling very good about me. It was almost like a movie star doing tons of films and then suddenly the producers saying, 'Sorry, dear, we don't need you in films anymore.'" But eventually as her children increased in their own capabilities, Margo had more time to do what she'll always enjoy: surfing.

I have been surfing a lot the last six months and have been really, really happy. I finally realized I wasn't doing anything for *me*. For about three years all I did was serve everybody else. I wanted to fulfill all my commitments at the Kiahuna Plantation, wanted to fulfill all my commitments to my kids, wanted to take care of Steve and what he was doing, and wanted to go to the women's Bible studies at church, and to listen to my friends when they called. I wanted, too, for Steve to listen to me and be considerate that I wanted a little bit more activity, like maybe one contest here or one promotion there. But I waited on the Lord for His leading, and I really felt He would always say, "I want you to stay home with the baby."

I'd rather hear "Margo is really dedicated to her kids and she really loves being a mom; she is really into that," because things like nurturing your family and making sacrifices are more internal—that's the way God deals with you. It's not really grumbling, but I thought being a parent would be a lot easier. I thought you do all these wonderful things for your kids—and we do—and then, I thought, they were going to be so appreciative. Shane will walk up sometimes and say, "I love you," or, "That was a great dinner. Make it again—I really like it." But other times it's, "You're making *that?*"

Part of me can really see why certain women have a hard time staying at home—because it is really a thankless job. Unless the husband compliments her efforts and appreciates her, no one would probably even notice or say thank you.

And the husband's life is more glamorous: lunch with the banker, tennis with his lawyer, flying over to Honolulu for business. The husband will come bursting in the door feeling good about a deal or how he's saved a client some big money on a day that the kids have gotten out every toy that you had already put away and little brother is yelling at big brother—you know, little things that are aggravating.

But with the Lord, you have positive benefits because you have a witness of why you are there: because God has a plan and calls us to be servants and to humble ourselves like Christ. But in a purely selfish state, you're asking yourself why you have to make such sacrifices. I don't know what the turning point was for me; probably the kids just getting a little older.

One morning at sunrise I was surfing and processing all that stuff in my mind and surrendering all my burdens, and I really felt like the Lord was giving me real peace about the gift of surfing He had given me. And I felt like He was telling me to just enjoy it and be happy about it.

Margo is banking that her long-term investments in her children will someday pay off with solid relationships.

My seven-year-old, I spent so much time with him that we are really, really close. Some kids might put up walls, but he is really open to me. We pray and sing at bedtime and I tickle him and we have fun. I really don't regret that I spend so much time with them. It's neat. I take them to the pool practically every day, and they swim, swim, swim.

In the Lord, I can see God's wisdom and planning, but if I wasn't a Christian I could see a rebellious root inside me—like when the woman has good ideas but the guys don't listen. I can see why some women who don't know the Lord and have a bad upbringing or experience with their dad can have some bitterness about getting a raw deal. I've met really intense women who would think it was just terrific if the whole planet was women. Sometimes with women like that you just don't see a lot of joy.

After Jason was born in 1987, Margo came back once again to place second in the 1988 World Cup event. No woman, even current world champion Frieda Zamba of Florida, can consistently beat Margo in the big Hawaiian surf.

I'll never regret that I got married and had kids, because I know that's exactly what God wanted me to do. But I did have to deal with the reality that I probably wouldn't be number one in the world anymore. But you never know—maybe God could just work a miracle and all the perfect waves would come right to me in a contest and all of a sudden I'd win again. There's a part of me that wishes I could travel and compete more. I'm just a little restless. I mean, some women can sit and watch TV or knit or do handiwork. I've got to stay physically active. Yet, I still really look forward to being with my little guys, my little kids.

If I could have traded those experiences for anything, or if somebody had said, "We'll give you anything you want materially in exchange," I still would have just said, "I'll take those same experiences."

I plan on staying in good enough shape to surf forever. Last night I went out on my big board, and realized I could go surfing on these long boards when my kids are in college and that's twenty years from now! I'll probably be the only lady surfing with gray hair!

And having been, I feel, obedient to God's priorities for family, I think there's a much better chance that my grown children will be among my best friends. The hope of that future blessing is sure worth any sacrifice I could make today.

# 3 *Betsy King*

## On the wings
## of an eagle

TO PRO GOLFER BETSY KING, there are paychecks and there are reality checks. From casual conversation it's clear she prefers the reality checks.

Winning the 1989 United States Women's Open meant a paycheck—$80,000—and fulfillment of a desire. How did she feel about that? "Okay," she says, as though unimpressed with herself. "I mean, it's so temporary and it just goes right on by. I really enjoy it while it's happening, but when it's over, it's over. People congratulate you and stuff, but when you have to get up at 5:00 A.M. the next morning to go to a junior golf camp," she pauses, "it's over." Those wee hours bring reality to anyone whether they're president of the United States, an office worker, or a pro golfer.

Winning the Open may be exciting, but Flamboyance is not Betsy's middle name. Nor is Artificial, Flashy, or Pompous. Low-key and steady, excitement to Betsy might be choosing the Jungle Fruit Sherbet or the Almond Roca Crunch instead of plain vanilla at Baskin-Robbins. Super excitement might be getting a scoop of each.

She's so unflappable and self-deprecating that she can shrug off potential embarrassments: like the time she sliced her finger open while trying to cut a bagel (the injury required stitches and nearly forced the defending champion out of the 1989 Rail Charity Classic in Springfield, Illinois). Or like the time she slipped on a floor rug while playing chase at her parents' home and wrenched her ankle so badly that she was forced off the tour for three weeks. Or like once when trying to correct a twelve-year-old girl's swing, she stood in the way of the golfer's follow-through and got hit, splitting her forehead near the hairline, badly enough to require plastic surgery.

"I stood behind her and bent her arm and told her to swing through, but I never moved so I got hit on the follow-through. I was lucky it was just a little kid. How much club speed can you have at ten or twelve years old?"

Certainly not as much as Betsy, although the youngster would do well to emulate her swing. In early August of a record-setting year for Betsy, she was the leading golfer in nearly every 1989 statistical category the Ladies Professional Golf Association publishes: Rolex Player of the Year; Vare Trophy (scoring average); Jamaica LPGA Series (cumulative standing); top ten finishes; number of birdies; number of rounds under par; and she was a close second to Nancy Lopez in scoring average: 70.34 to 70.72, which was still Betsy's career best. She was also on her way to setting an LPGA record for most rounds in the 60s.

A superstar in her field who makes beaucoup bucks for things like endorsing certain golf courses in Japan and for wearing manufacturer's labels on her visor and bag, Betsy is nevertheless unaffected and unpretentious. It's just no big deal. When the public forgets about the tournaments she's won and the celebrities she's met and the money she's made, Betsy realizes she'll still have to live with herself. So why get carried away?

Those close to her, like junior golf camp director Captain Bill Lewis, call the 5-foot-6-inch blue-eyed blonde "genuine." She's into playing the organ, visiting the theatre, and listening to soft music nearly as much as she's into golf. Her parents had the right idea when they enrolled her at Furman, a small, conservative and academically demanding university (enrollment 2,500) outside Greenville, South Carolina. Classes were a short walk away on the lovely, wooded 750-acre campus, bordered by the golf course. Betsy, one of nine Furman grads on the LPGA Tour, studied more than just course layouts and greens, graduating cum laude in physical education in 1977.

Betsy remains close to her alma mater and, along with Beth Daniel, has partially endowed a permanent golf scholarship there. Since 1981 she's hosted a Pro/Am fundraiser for Furman, inviting twenty-six of her fellow female pros, which has raised upwards of $50,000 each spring for the women's golf program and endowment.

While at Furman, Betsy also played basketball, but "We were pitiful," she says, and describes a game against the University of

Tennessee that the "Purple Paladins" lost by seventy points. "I'm not that tall, and I was playing forward because we didn't have anyone else. It really changed my outlook, going from playing on a winning high school team to one that gets slapped down all the time." After putting the ball in the hoop collegiately for three years and spending a lot of time rehabilitating a knee injury, she gradually concerted her efforts on smaller balls, longer shots, and smaller holes, and somehow still increased her proficiency.

She still greatly enjoys basketball, and the outlet it provides for releasing tension. "I mean, you can get up in your opponent's face and play a little defense if things aren't going so well," she says as if from experience.

> You can't do that in golf. You can't get that emotional. I think you can't help being emotional, but it works against you if you are. They say the finer the skill, the less emotional you should be. For instance if you compare sewing with a needle to football, which is a large muscle skill, then you realize in football you have to get all pumped up. But can you imaging getting all hyped up and trying to sew?

That steadiness has helped Betsy to win more than twenty official LPGA titles (along with the Women's British Open and a Japanese event) and 2.5 million dollars in prize money as she has successfully modified her competitive drive to meet the needs of golf.

Furman University, founded in 1826, is a Southern Baptist institution where attendance at a weekly chapel is required. Betsy dutifully attended, although she says, the chapel really wasn't a religious service. "On Wednesday mornings they had what they called a 'Religion in Life' course, where they brought in speakers like Dr. Joyce Brothers and former President Jimmy Carter. It was more of a humanities type thing." Some students wanted Betsy to become involved in their evening Bible studies, but disinterested at the time, she politely declined. She thought it was pretty strange to see posters for Bible studies in her dorm's hallways.

Having been raised in a mainline denominational church where "no one brings their Bible," she says religion just wasn't a priority to her. She'd passed her church's confirmation classes and felt that was the end of it.

However, after graduating from Furman and getting her LPGA tour card she began to analyze what she felt was a disturbing tendency to fluctuate emotionally according to her performance on the course. Betsy had enjoyed some good times, sure, helping

Furman win the Association of Intercollegiate Athletics for Women national title in 1976. Later that same summer she had earned a top-eight finish at the U.S. Women's Open as an amateur, the best by a non-pro in ten years. Yet Betsy wasn't happy with her inconsistencies.

At a 1979 Fellowship of Christian Athletes Golf Day in Florida, Betsy had an opportunity to question some of the women about their faith—women like current pro Donna White, 1962 U.S. Open winner Murle Breer, and soon-to-be tour chaplain Margie Davis. "Just because you're not a Christian doesn't mean you can't play in the tournament. They have a dinner afterwards with a speaker who shares what Christ means to him or her," Betsy points out. Ever studious, she carefully analyzed what she heard.

A few weeks later, Margie invited Betsy to a Tee-Off Conference designed around playing golf and learning what it means to have a personal relationship with the Lord. Betsy was attracted by the afternoon practice time as much as the morning and evening general sessions. "I figured the worst that could happen would be that I could work on my game, because I had never been to these fellowship things."

At the conference's close, the speaker, Bruce Wilkinson from a ministry called "Walk Through the Bible," offered the golfers an opportunity to pray and invite Christ into their lives. Betsy, after careful consideration, did that. "I had never heard before how to invite Christ into your life."

Perhaps there weren't any immediate evident outward changes because, as Betsy says, "I've never been that wild so it's not like I had to give up drugs or anything like that."

Betsy grew up in Reading, Pennsylvania, fifty-five miles northwest of Philadelphia. Her father, Weir, a doctor, and her mother, Helen, a homemaker, along with older brother Lee, lived in a spacious country house atop a hill surrounded by thirty-plus acres of rolling hills. Looking out the front, there's a view across nearly fifteen miles of the valley. Betsy's parents, both avid golfers, started Betsy in the sport when she was ten. An all-around athlete, she also played softball, basketball, and field hockey, competing in golf tournaments during summers only.

By fifteen, she had entered the U.S. Golf Association Junior Nationals at Augusta, Georgia, but failed to make the final round of thirty. Two years later when she beat central Pennsylvania golf standout Betty Fehl, who was thirty years older, for a Central Pennsylvania title, Betsy began to realize she might have some real potential as a golfer. Finally, in 1973 a few weeks before leaving for Furman, she made the semifinals at the USGA Junior Girls Championship. Amy Alcott took the title and turned professional shortly afterward.

While some athletes may crave attention, Betsy certainly does not. She's aware that because of her success people look at her as a celebrity. "I don't really look at myself as being a celebrity," she says. "I mean, I hate being asked to sign autographs. I don't think I would ever ask anyone for an autograph because I think it demeans the person. It's like you see them as more of a *thing* than a person." Once a fan asked for her autograph but didn't have a pen or anything for her to sign. Brazenly, he asked for one of her golf gloves!

Humility seasons Betsy's character. She'd rather serve than be served. That attitude has been more consistent than even her golf swing.

For the past few years for a week each October, she trades in her soft garment-leather golf gloves for rough leather work gloves and pounds nails while helping in the LPGA Fellowship's work project and Habitat for Humanity. Up to a dozen female pros join tour chaplain Cris Stevens in Tennessee's Appalachian Mountains to build housing for the poor. "It's something so different from golf. I won't even take my clubs along. It's nice not to travel with them," she says, joking about how the golfers change the focus of their competitiveness from swinging golf clubs to swinging hammers and driving nails. "We have a lot of fun just being together and working together, but we still try to compete to see who's driving the most nails or getting the most work done."

She also gives her time to the LPGA Fellowship Group's children's church.

During the fellowship time [the Thursday night prior to a tournament's opening] we started a children's program and the single players take turns teaching the kids. Each week two different players do it. There might be a maximum of five kids, but it's been really good for them and for their parents to be able to come.

So how did Betsy, who is single, do in her stint with the kids in Atlantic City?

Betsy laughs heartily. "I was a bust." Would watching a pair of two-year-olds contribute to that? "I was trying to follow a curriculum for five-year-olds, but I knew that wouldn't work so we just

colored something." Good idea. No seasoned mother would have
done differently.

Don't expect to see Betsy on TV hawking all her memorabilia
like many athletes. And if there were golf card conventions like
there are baseball card conventions, you wouldn't see Betsy there,
either. However, she says, she may do appearances just to fulfill a
contract, like the time in Japan when she sat at a department store
and signed away. At least she has a short name. What if her
parents had called her Elizabeth?

Although such appearances may seem like an opportunity to
tell others about her faith in God, Betsy waits for better chances
to share. She says that she has a hard time herself with the wit-
nessing of others unless they can back up what they are saying by
the way they live. "Strangers would have no impact on me," she
says. "Take, for instance, the guy who flashes the John 3:16 sign
all the time at sporting events and tries to get on camera: I think,
if anything, people get turned off with that approach."

Betsy is also considerate of the media in not continually pushing
her Christian faith. As often as those reporters have seen Betsy in
the media tent after all her wins, it would get old pretty fast.

> I don't always go in there and say something about God, because I
> want to be seen as a real person not some religious whacko. When
> you spend as much time as I do with the media, it's not like every
> single time I have to share something. I think I get a lot of respect for
> that. Sometimes, the reporters who might be Christians even bring
> up my trust in God by asking leading questions like how I maintain
> inner peace on the course.
>
> It's not like every time I open my mouth I have to talk about my
> faith. People are curious about you when you're successful and want
> to know why, and I try to let that speak for itself. Others look at your
> life: what you say and what you're doing and it has to be consistent.
> Other players too can see how you are on the golf course, how
> you act. Everybody sometimes "loses it" out there. I know I get upset
> sometimes, but not really mad, and I've certainly gotten better about
> handling my emotions.

So, the changes in Betsy's life weren't outward so much as
inward, having to do with personal traits like achievement, comparison, and self-control. She's still achievement-oriented, but in
a different way than before.

Betsy explains. In 1981, she heard a speaker define goals and
desires, and she reevaluated her career in those terms.

He said you should never have a goal that you don't have total control over in achieving. That really changed my perspective. Before that I would go out and say, "My goal is to win the Open and my goal is to win a hundred thousand dollars this year."

But you don't have complete control over that because everybody else is out there trying to do the same thing. He'd describe marriage counseling where a spouse would say, "My goal is to have a good marriage." That's not a good goal, he said, because it's not dependent on *you* entirely. The proper goal in that situation would be trying to be the best marriage partner you can be no matter what the other person is doing.

A desire, he said, is something you would like to achieve but you realize you don't have 100 percent control over. Perhaps your desire would be wanting to have a good marriage.

Finally, he said to take responsibility for your goals and pray about your desires.

As Betsy evaluates that in regard to golf, she says her goal is to be 100 percent prepared for every tournament. "That's something I can control in terms of working on my game and being mentally ready: taking lessons and giving 100 percent on every shot on the golf course. I like to say I'm maximizing my chances for success.

"That's the only thing I can control. I can't control what everyone else is doing and how well they're playing."

Focusing on her goals seems to have led to the fulfillment of Betsy's desires as well. In 1989, she won six tournament titles beginning with the Jamaica Classic in January and the televised win at the Nestlé World Championship in Buford, Georgia. The U.S. Open win, her second major title, pushed her official earnings over $500,000 in a single season, the first woman to do so. That year Betsy also claimed the Nestlé World Championship against the best sixteen players from around the world (like Juli Inkster, Nancy Lopez, Beth Daniel, and Patty Sheehan).

If her parents had had foresight they would have named her Betty, not Betsy; as in Steady Betty. "It's hard to play well all the time in golf, and I have just really not gone through any kind of slump this year [1989], which is pretty amazing," she says. Betsy's not praising herself here, just stating the facts. She quickly goes on to mention how she nearly broke her consecutive string of top-ten finishes in Seattle by being three shots away from the top ten, but then pulled through with a final-day score of 66 to finish fourth.

Prestige + Promotions + Praise + Press = Pressure? Not to Betsy.

To Betsy pressure would be disappointing seventy youngsters at the FCA junior golf camp the day after winning the U.S. Open. So at 7:45 A.M. on the morning of the final round of the Open, she was contacting camp director Captain Bill Lewis in Indianapolis to confirm her travel plans.

"On a day so important to her, there she was checking to make sure I knew her flight plans," the seventy-year-old retired navy captain marvels.

While smoothing travel plans may have been foremost on her mind, Betsy's phone call to Captain Lewis could have been to seek some sage wisdom from a mentor she's known ten years and whom she calls her "second dad." Betsy, tied with Patty Sheehan for the lead going into the last eighteen holes, birdied three of the first four holes to finish three under par.

Captain Bill describes how less than twenty-four hours later, on Monday afternoon, Betsy was on the camp golf course giving four young golfers the thrill of their lives by playing a round with them in the opening tournament which is called "Captain's Choice." (The golf pro is the captain, and plays with four amateurs of mixed handicaps. After all tee off, the captain selects the best drive, and all play that ball.) Betsy spent two and a half days teaching techniques, carting kids to their tees, joining their small group Bible discussions, and speaking about her faith in Christ.

It was an opportunity to keep her Promises, fulfill her Principles, demonstrate her Priorities. She could easily have said that she was too tired from the Open, that it was emotionally draining and the interviews and media responsibilities were too demanding. But this was vintage Betsy, thinking beyond herself.

Indeed on the golf course, she's always thinking one or two shots ahead, sort of like playing on a giant chess board. In 1989 she once again proved she was a master player on golf's giant green chess board by winning her second Rolex Player of the Year Award (the first was in 1984).

Betsy has improved consistently since 1977, her first year on the tour, when she played eight events and won only $4,008. That hardly covers travel expenses today, but it was a beginning. She consistently averaged $46,000 in winnings over the next five years before jumping up to nearly $95,000 in 1983. With her stroke average dropping steadily (from 74.46 in 1977 to 72.88 in 1983 to her career low of 71.14 in 1987 when she won over

$460,000), Betsy picked up her first tournament wins in 1984: Women's Kemper Open, Freedom Orlando Classic, Columbia Savings Classic. Those championships helped her clinch that season's Rolex Player of the Year Award.

Being a Christian has modified her inward character in other ways. Betsy's learned to be competitive against the course rather than her opponents. Not long after she had accepted Christ, she was playing in a tournament alongside Laura Baugh. One particular hole was disastrous for Betsy: she twice hit the ball out of bounds, taking penalty strokes, and finishing with a 10 on the hole and a 76 for the round. Later in the locker room Laura was overheard saying, "I can't believe Betsy King. She made a 10 out there and didn't even get mad!" Although the extra shots were uncharacteristic, Betsy's response was not.

*Los Angeles Times* columnist Jim Murray says she has the best two instruction books written: the Old and New Testaments. "They don't tell you how to hit a wood over water," he once wrote. "But they tell you what to do when the shot doesn't come off. Smile. And go on to the next one."[1]

It might further surprise people to know Betsy regularly encourages other players by sincerely complimenting their efforts.

Lots of times players can't acknowledge good play by others because they feel threatened. I think it surprises people when I say encouraging things. You can root for them and still try like crazy to beat them.

I concentrate and work hard when I'm on the golf course, but away from there, I've been getting to know different players. Maybe we'll go out to dinner, and sometimes I share what the Lord means to me personally. Sometimes it's easier to invite someone to the Christian Golf Fellowship than to approach them and ask if they've received Christ. In golf there's an unspoken rule about never telling another player what to do. If I'm trying to remain that equal [person], then if I come on as though I'm better than someone else they'll wonder "Who are you to tell me how to live my life or to do this or that?"

People have this big thing about saying they don't need "religion." The bottom line for me is that this isn't religion, it's *truth*. I really believe that. That's why I made a decision for Christ, not because I wasn't doing okay or because I was really messed up, into drugs or something. It wasn't like I wasn't going to get by in life. Sometimes Christianity is presented as a way to success, or a way to solve problems, or just a way to get by.

---

1. *Los Angeles Times*, 2 April 1989; III 1:1.

But it begins by the fact that it's truth. Jesus said, "I am the way, and the truth, and the life; no one comes to the Father, but through Me" (John 14:6). That's where faith should begin.

Her steady faith and excellent reputation have given her a platform to address a sensitive issue often linked with female athletes: homosexuality. A January 1989 *Sports Illustrated* article on the LPGA tour's problems called it the "Lesbian Professional Golf Association" and hinted that "gay women outnumbered straight women on the tour."[2] Those not involved with that lifestyle were somewhat stung by the inference of guilt by association.

"It's not like the tennis circuit, where Martina Navratilova has admitted openly to it. There hasn't been one player on our tour who has come out and said, 'I'm gay and I'm proud of it.' They might *think* that but there's nobody who's come out and said that, so it's still an unspoken issue," says Betsy, not denying its presence on the LPGA tour, yet willing to reach out to those involved.

Everybody knows that the LPGA Fellowship doesn't think it's right, but that doesn't prevent anyone from coming to the meetings. We welcome all players, husbands, caddies, and those associated with the tour to come and learn about the person of Jesus Christ.

Some of those players have come, but you know, if you don't change your life and begin to follow the Lord, usually you fall out of fellowship and don't want to be around other Christians. Either one or the other goes—your lifestyle or your faith in God. God is a forgiving God, but there are certain responsibilities we have to take.

Betsy has to deal with controversy about the LPGA in her public life, yet her private life is orderly and refreshing. Superstar here does not translate to Super-Ego. When visiting her desert home in Scottsdale, Arizona, minutes northeast of Phoenix, you'd never know you were entering the home of an outstanding professional golfer. Tastefully furnished inside with big comfy sofas, out back the closely clipped grass invites a few practice putts. She talks a little about herself, but she'd rather show you how others have noted her career. On first glancing around the living room you'd probably miss the beautiful, but unobtrusive Vare Trophy (for lowest scoring average). And you'd certainly never know from the visible evidence that she was pro golf's nominee for Sportswoman of the Year.

---

2. "Find the Golf Here?" *Sports Illustrated*, vol. 70, no. 7 (13 February 1989).

If you visited the back room, a combination library and TV room equipped with both a Nintendo and a Lifecycle, you'd see over twenty beautifully framed articles from golf magazines color-fully highlighting each of her tour victories. She wouldn't show you the many accolades except to praise the work done by an older gentleman. She'll point out on the bookshelves the Japanese deco-rative leather scrapbooks inlaid with gold metallic designs because of their uniqueness, not because they're filled with testimonies to her personal glory.

Sure, winning the 1989 U.S. Open and the Player of the Year Award was satisfying, but beyond that, Betsy sees her remarkable consistency as her greatest achievement in golf.

"There's not really one thing I'd say, except that the hardest thing is to be consistent," she says, noting that for the past six years she's always been ranked in the top ten. During that time she's also won more tournaments than any other professional golfer, male or female.

> The reason is that I'm always trying to give 100 percent. A lot of people get burned out a lot quicker than I do. For instance in Philip-pians it talks about forgetting what is behind and straining toward what is ahead. I know that is talking in terms of faith, but in golf that's also one of the most important things. Whatever has happened on the hole behind you, you have to forget it whether it's good or bad, and be right on the present.

Even if you have a good hole you can't get so excited," she says and describes one round where she was 7 under par after only twelve holes, and then played too conservatively, trying to shoot only par. "You have to be able to put that behind you. Golfers talking at night will say, 'Oh that shot on the fourth hole just ruined my day.' It's really hard to put that consistently behind you. But you have to. And you can't compare yourself with others."

She's so purposeful that right now she can't imagine playing just for fun. "It's not so much like a job that I don't enjoy it, but I just can't see coming out to play eighteen holes just for fun. Not being able to play the way I want to play might be frustrating. Maybe I'll change when I get to be fifty or sixty."

Watch out then, sports fans, for a future LPGA Seniors Tour!

# 4

# *Wendy White*

## Winner in the
## King's court

WENDY WHITE CAN WIN a lot of things—her parents knew
something when they put lots of W's in her name—but she
couldn't win the couch-potato decathlon.

She wouldn't excel at the major league sport of rotting.

She couldn't master even the minor league sport of rotting.

Rotting is defined in professional baseball lore as the "art of
doing absolutely nothing" (always double the t, please). That's an
art form understandable to many but beyond her comprehension
and feeble experience. She's too active. She's definitely not in
the mold of the cartoon character Garfield. That cat could rott
the day away. Not Wendy.

From her birth on September 29, 1960, to the present, professional tennis player Wendy White has had too many places to go,
people to meet, and things to see. Life's fun, a great big Peter Pan
adventure of flying the globe, dueling her Captain Hooks across a
tennis net. You can't prosper on the pro tennis circuit by rotting
on the top side of the family sofa. There's simply no time.

"I was always involved in sports: Basketball when I was seven,
eight, and nine, and competitive swimming, too," she says,
dressed in jams and a T-shirt while relaxing between matches in
a prestigious $250,000 women's professional tournament in
Manhattan Beach, California. "My parents weren't very athletic,
but they were always real supportive of my interest in sports.
Because I was so energetic, they always found good outlets for
me—mainly sports—to release my energy. I was into anything
that required any type of exertion." That's definitely an anti-rott
attitude. And it began early.

Indeed, when she was eight, her parents, Phil and Nancy, packed Wendy up and sent her from hometown Atlanta to a summer camp in Alabama, hoping two weeks of horseback riding, sports, and water activities might soak up her youthful enthusiasm. Instead of being worn out like her parents expected, she exuberantly returned home with added excitement from discovering a new sport: tennis. It was a fresh challenge and she loved it.

"When I got back home from camp, my parents saw to it that I had lessons at a local club," she says, recalling the first courts she played on. "But I first learned at that camp, on this old court with grass and roots sticking out of the asphalt and this big tree trunk in the middle. Nothing special really." Playing there added new meaning to "keep your eyes on the ball" and "that's the way the ball bounces." With a little more grass, a little less asphalt, and a girl's imagination it could be good practice for Wimbledon, the premier grass-court tennis event in London, England!

Despite less than ideal conditions ("Out! That serve was on the root."), Wendy and a group of her friends began competing across the state of Georgia in various tournaments for their age, advancing to Southern regional tournaments, and even to nationals by the time Wendy was fourteen.

Tennis was king in her life, and she was the local queen of the court. But when Wendy enrolled at private Westminster High School in Atlanta, she began to learn what it meant to put tennis in proper perspective and to have a personal relationship with the Lord.

"My high school wasn't affiliated with a church but you had to take classes like Old Testament and New Testament," recounts the outgoing athlete. "We studied the Bible a lot. I had a teacher named Drew Trotter who was a believer, and he had a real strong influence on me. In his class I first began to understand what the Bible meant. I just had never read it."

Wendy describes hearing various people who visited her school and shared testimonies about what Christ meant in their lives. She also participated in weekly Friday assemblies and singing. But tennis, dating, and school activities were still at the center of her life, not God. Jesus was a sort of good luck charm—in her life but not influencing her decisions. Wendy says she was looking at what God could do for her, rather than who He really is.

There were also Bible study and prayer groups that met outside of school hours. "My mother used to always want me to go to the Bible studies, but I never could because of tennis," says the perky brown-eyed blonde with the Pepsodent smile. "I'd always believed in God, but I was always looking to God to meet *my* specific desires, especially in tennis."

Wendy's mother frequently left Christian literature around, hoping to arouse Wendy's interest in spiritual things—books like Harold Hill's *How to Be a King's Kid* and, of course, the Bible. "Mom was definitely a big influence. I just read as much as I could, books that were about the Lord and had Scripture. And I had a Bible that I'd read. I didn't understand much. But I remember trying to.

"And, too, I remember praying a lot. 'How do I deal with this match and that match?'" Once a nervous Wendy even called the 700 Club, a nationally televised Christian program on CBN, seeking to gain reassurance prior to a tough match in the eighteen-and-under nationals by soliciting prayer support. They prayed. Wendy played.

> I don't even remember how I did. I think I won. But more importantly, I felt a peace. At that time I was just totally afraid. A lot of me was wanting to trust the Lord, but I felt like I was just giving Him tennis, because that's where I felt totally inadequate. But as I trusted God with my tennis, I could see that whatever I let go of to Him, I prospered in.

Despite her success as a four-time AA state champion and honor roll student, she felt inadequate *and* intimidated. There were lots of reasons to play tennis—she enjoyed the game, the travel, different situations, meeting new people, the competition. Although she reigned as the top Georgia player for four years, Wendy was relatively unknown beyond the state line. And she knew if she was going to improve she would have to seek tougher competition. For her, it was sort of like going from being Shamu at Sea World to being a tuna at Starkist.

"I was at the bottom of the ladder on the national circuit," she recalls, explaining how greatly she enjoyed the game and wanted to compete at the highest level possible with her God-given talent. "I never pursued tennis for the recognition it could give me or money or any other thing, because I didn't really care about those things. It was just a good release for me and my personality."

Indeed, Wendy enjoyed the game so much that it began to rule her life. She was involved in a few outside activities, but nothing eclipsed the importance of tennis. "I had a lot going for me, a good variety of things—a great family, a church I enjoyed, a boyfriend. Everything seemed to be fitting into place naturally," the former high school star says today. While tennis success continued to dominate her life, spiritually she sensed an inner emptiness needing to be filled.

At age sixteen she received an invitation to try out in Houston for the Junior Wightman Cup. Positions were available to ten upcoming young talents who would be sponsored by the United States Tennis Association to travel to various competitions. Though outstanding in her own right, Wendy felt overwhelmed by the big-name players from Southern California, Florida, and Texas—Tracy Austin and Pam Shriver, Kathy Jordan (who later was to beat Wendy for an Association of Intercollegiate Athletics for Women national title), Mary Lou Piatek (now Daniels), "Peanut" Louie Harper, and Barbara Potter. They were all seasoned veterans, though they were all still eighteen and under, and they, too, were seeking to represent the United States internationally.

Wendy had performed well in previous tryouts, yet she felt her opponents were skeptical of her talent, as though scoffing, "Who's this little dinky Southern girl from Atlanta and what can *she* do?"

Those negative thoughts kept replaying like a scratched record. Feelings of insecurity and inadequacy surfaced. Wendy deeply wanted to make the team but doubted her own potential. One moment she was confident, listening to the still small voice that predicted success; the next moment, she was unsure.

Finally, the still small voice of confidence won.

"It shocked me when I got on the team," she says, adding that her name was the last called that particular day. "Not that God always has to show Himself in our victories and advances. He can work through our defeats and disappointments. But at that time I was really growing in my trust in the Lord and looking to the Lord more in everyday situations in my life rather than just a shallow 'Hey, I believe in God.' It was satisfying to realize, 'This is where God wants me.'"

With those honors—the state high school championships, being eighth-ranked American junior tennis player, and making the Junior Wightman Cup—etched on her racket, Wendy pondered college opportunities. Numerous schools sought the 5-foot-7-inch senior's services—along with her overheads, passing shots, and volleys. She selected tiny Rollins College in Winter Park,

Florida, which had about as many students as a UCLA freshman lecture class, and yet boasted a proud tradition in women's tennis, topped by former pro Nancy Yeargin.

In the postseason AIAW tennis nationals, Rollins, a thirteen-hundred-student liberal arts institution, rolled to third place, highlighted by defeating UCLA in match play. The team finished right behind USC and Stanford. In the individual competition, Wendy finished second overall to Kathy Jordan. That year she represented the U.S. in the Junior Federation Cup (for amateur players in their first or second year of college) and the Maureen Connolly Cup played against Great Britain, and dabbled in a few professional tournaments.

The next season, 1980, Rollins slipped to fifth nationally, but Wendy won the individual national title, garnering the Broderick Award in collegiate tennis and being tabbed by *Tennis Magazine* as the "College Player of the Year."

Wendy's collegiate success gave her confidence and experience, and Wendy sensed that she was ready for a professional career. Entering tournaments as a pro, the reigning collegiate champion catapulted to wins that summer over the top ten players. A significant event in her career was when she defeated the legendary Billie Jean King, who was then closing her career. She also beat Virginia Ruzici and Helena Sukova and raised her ranking to number 22.

For the next two years Wendy entered tournaments infrequently while she finished her business communications degree. After Wendy graduated with honors in 1982 she became a full-time pro, but saw her ranking slide with the addition of more tournaments to her schedule.

"I wasn't doing much of anything different but because I was playing more tournaments my ranking went down. Generally in my career I've been in the top fifty (which earns her a position in almost any tournament draw without having to go through the pretournament qualifying). I've had a couple of slumps where I ranked in the nineties, and I'm at that point right now." Rankings fluctuate frequently, and in closing out the 1989 season, Wendy was on the rise. After winning the Ladies Plate at Wimbledon (a sort of consolation tournament for first and second round losers), Wendy and doubles partner Mary Lou Daniels reached the semifinals of the United Jersey Bank Classic in Mahwah, New Jersey before losing to eventual champions Steffi Graf and Pam Shriver. Wendy also defeated number 10 seed Mary Joe

Fernandez at the U.S. Open in September to boost her ranking and her confidence in overcoming a serious illness which previously had affected her.

In August of 1987, Wendy had contracted mononucleosis. Her ranking had climbed back into the twenties at number 28, and the twenty-six-year-old seemed poised to make an impact.

"I went to a doctor to get diagnosed because I felt really exhausted, much more than I'd ever felt before. He told me that a lot of athletes get mono, and that healing was just a process and that I needed to keep pressing through it. But the more I pressed the more exhausted I was." Recovery could be from six weeks to a year or more, according to the individual case. Wendy went the full route. "For me, it took literally a full year to get through it."

Her illness was compounded by exhaustion from the grind of weekly tournaments—adjusting to different time zones and climates (hot and humid to cool and clammy), foreign countries and irregular eating situations, getting into town and immediately hitting the practice courts, getting ready, competing. "All that together can make it real tough on you."

Wendy is cautious about discussing her money winnings, preferring not to discuss it because monetary figures can be so misleading. Yet according to the Women's International Tennis Association, Wendy has $500,000-plus in career earnings in her ten-year career, winning over $50,000 of that in 1988. She's sponsored by Reebok, is also a member of the Pringle's Light Brigade (a team concept sponsored by Pringle's Light Potato Chips in conjunction with the WITA) and made the 1988 Lipton/WITA calendar.

She's content and has earned a good living off the tour, and her tennis clothing and racket sponsors give her free equipment. Once or twice a year she visits her clothing and shoe supplier and exits with the latest styles and designs. For her, there's no cash and carry. It's all carry. For sweatsuit junkies, it would be the overdose of a lifetime.

"It's a good living, but nothing extravagant. It definitely was better than anything else I could have gotten going right out of college!" she says. In other words, Wendy is making more than a secretary but less than a neurosurgeon, and having more fun than either. A big payday for Wendy might be small change to Steffi Graf, Martina Navratilova, or Chris Evert, but it's enough to keep Wendy happy.

I had a friend, a guy who asked me what I earned and he offered a guess which was totally unrealistic. I just collapsed, laughing, "You've got to be kidding!" When you see figures in the paper about prize money and such, most of it is going to the top, those in the top five or top ten. They are the ones with sponsors' insignia on their clothing, with contracts on everything from sunglasses to watches to fast food to soft drinks.

Women's tennis today offers more prize money than ever before, but racket companies and tennis-wear manufacturers are feeling the squeeze of the economy. Mom's at aerobics class and Dad's on his bike. Tennis companies are bankrolling one or two players while designing other contracts that give players performance-based bonuses—kind of like a merit raise at the end of the year for reaching certain levels.

Down-to-earth and practical, yet sophisticated enough to wend her way around the globe from Tokyo to Paris to London, Wendy makes her own travel arrangements, often staying with friends in cities where she's playing (but more for the fellowship than the opportunity to cut hotel expenses). The top handful of tennis pros may have traveling entourages complete with a nutritionist, trainer, masseur, and psychologist to attend to their needs, but not Wendy. She's on her own, with only a part-time coach to prepare her for matches.

She's part press agent, accountant, and travel agent—this working girl *really* works! When they call from Raleigh and it's 6:00 P.M. and they need a player for 10:00 A.M. the next day, she gets on the phone herself, exercising her fingers dialing the airlines. If she's available, she'll try to make the connection by flying the "Red-Eye Express."

If Wendy could be compared to a car, it definitely would not be a Ferrari Testarossa—powerful, sleek, and hands off. She's too much like a warm bouncy puppy for that. The Testarossa would be Martina Navratilova.

Nor is it a Rolls Royce Silver Shadow—elegant and royal. She's too spontaneous for that. That would be Chris Evert.

No, she's definitely the Jeep C-J7 with the roof down, practical, approachable, durable, fun-loving, and sun-loving. And she's fueled by the most powerful engine of all—an *eternal* combustion engine. And with her faith in Jesus Christ, she's looking beyond rankings and prize winnings.

Despite the travels and stress of competition in an occupation where "every day there's a winner and a loser," Wendy has seen one thing in her life remain consistent: her relationship with Christ. She says,

Some might think I'm overspiritualizing, but I look to the Lord definitely as my Lord and Savior, and also as my comfort, my strength, and my closest friend. No matter where I go, He's there. I do have a great family that supports me; there are certain relationships and certain friends that I've had all these years. I'd say my relationships are consistent, and the number one relationship is that relationship with the Lord.

After getting her degree from Rollins in 1982, Wendy moved back to Atlanta for a few years, then to Ft. Worth, Texas. A handful of other players have called "Cowtown" their home, most notably Martina Navratilova. Wendy could have based herself in almost any city, but felt like God was directing her to Ft. Worth. "I live there because the Lord led me—because I never would have picked it out on a map!" More upscale Dallas, perhaps; or Disney's Magic Kingdom in Orlando, Florida. But Ft. Worth?

I like being in Ft. Worth, and I like its being more low key. I can go in to Dallas when I want to, where there are a whole lot of ministries available for me to get involved with.

I've gotten plugged into a church, a very small church of about two hundred, and it's almost like another family to me, a spiritual family. And that's provided a lot of consistency, I've found.

It's real important to be under the covering of a local body, getting to know other people in your church and your pastors. They know when I'm coming in and when I'm going out. They write. They call. I call them. When I'm there they always want me to get up and say what's going on.

They pray for people on the circuit. We have a whole bulletin board at the church with different tennis players' names listed and what their needs are.

Wendy frequently invites visiting tennis players to her home, especially the foreign players who may have a break in their schedules and nowhere to go. It's an opportune mission field and Wendy and her housemates, who include other athletes and former tennis players, often extend a welcome.

A lot of players don't have a place to call their home away from home, especially the foreign girls. We say, "Come and stay a few days

with us. We'll practice (we live right next to Texas Christian University and it has a great tennis facility), have fun, and you can go to
church with us. Basically, just come and be refreshed." Players need
that, a place where they can go and just be themselves. We've kind of
set our household aside for that.

We want to provide a place where they can just relax and see that
Christians are just as normal as anyone else, but where they can also
be ministered to. A lot of times it's easier to relate to them off the
circuit, away from a tournament. It's hard to sit and have good talks
with people at tournaments because there are schedule changes and
practice times and different lengths of times for matches.

Home can mean many things to different people, but to Wendy,
home is where the racket is.

Author's note: Wendy married Scott Prausa May 12, 1990, in Ft. Worth.

ABOVE: Betsy King, 1989 LPGA
Player of the Year
RIGHT: Margo Oberg, Women's
World Champion of Surfing seven

Basketball Entertainer Tanya
Crevier

ABOVE: Professional Tennis Player
Wendy White
LEFT: Four-Time Track Olympian
Madeline Manning Mims

Professional Softball Pitcher
Rosie Black of the Queen
and Her Court

# 5

# *Tanya Crevier*

## Hoop, hoop, hooray!

SPELLBOUND, 125 ELEMENTARY SCHOOL KIDS sit watching a morning assembly, fascinated by the performer on stage. She's Tanya Crevier, the "World's Finest Female Basketball Handler," according to posters and brochures. This unique title is a mouthful, but how else do you describe the ballhandling maneuvers she displays?

Music begins and Tanya starts the kids clapping rhythmically in time to the music. They don't know what to expect, but in the next thirty minutes they'll see some incredible feats. Tanya sets the ball atop one finger, and one youngster whispers to another, "Oh, my dad can do that!"

But then Tanya walks the ball down her fingertips and tosses it into the air, around her back, under her arms, while she does a 360-degree turn, all the while keeping the ball spinning. She juggles first one basketball, then two, three, and four. She throws three balls in the air in a straight horizontal line and catches them in a straight horizontal line. Up they go together and together they come down. Bet the kid's dad can't do that. Or her one-handed cartwheel while spinning a ball in the other hand. The basketball-lady nails her routine. The boy strains to take in everything as the show accelerates.

Grab the video camera; leave the Instamatic at home. What follows can only be captured in motion. Roll the tape because photos and words don't do justice. Balls blur as they whiz by. Up and down, in and out; finally she pauses, balancing the ball as it sits stationary on her index finger. The kids sit fascinated. They like it all.

It's the same everywhere Tanya performs: schools, basketball camps, National Basketball Association half times, college games, prisons, even her aunt's nursing home in Cherokee, Iowa. Audiences love the enthusiastic, inspiring thirty-four-year-old former professional basketball player. The twinkle in her eyes ought to be captured and put on a gold ring.

Tanya is to basketball what Ivory is to soap—99.4 percent pure—and filled with enthusiasm, too. For the next thirty minutes, she'll touch these kids' lives with a message beyond basketball.

Her performance is strictly G-rated—for GOOD. She's wholesome enough to do a milk commercial. And being a midwest farmer's daughter, she'd probably even be able to milk the cow. The fifth child in a family of eleven—after Maurice, Marc, Teresa, and Ray, Jr., and before Karen, Beth, Bert, Ann, Bruce, and Janine—Tanya learned early to follow in her father's steps by doing outside chores around the Crevier's six-bedroom farmhouse in Jefferson, South Dakota.

Somehow, her parents always found time to make each child feel special. Raymond and Patricia Crevier also taught the kids to entertain themselves, purchasing plenty of basketballs, footballs, and baseballs for whatever was in season. "Can you imagine all the games—not only football, basketball, and track, but all the other things we kids were participating in—that they had to attend?" Tanya asks. "And somehow they made each one of us feel like we were winners. Although the competition in my family was fierce sometimes, we were each able to experience our own amount of success a certain amount of the time."

All of Tanya's older siblings were an inspiration to her through their success and dedication in athletics and music. "I wanted to be just like them, and so I started practicing basketball. I would pretty much do the things they would do whenever they were home, whether it was the piano or sports."

As she performs, Tanya encourages the youths to work hard in the same way and to develop the talents God has given them, whether in music or math or myriad other things. She tells them that when she would get discouraged trying to learn new tricks, God would give her the desire to continue practicing and would bring encouragers to her. And she tells them the ABCD's of following in her Heavenly Father's footsteps: she *Admitted* to God that she was a sinner (Romans 3:23); she *Believed* in God (Romans 10:9); she *Confessed* Jesus Christ as Savior (1 John 1:9);

and she *Did it*, acted upon her beliefs (John 1:12) and invited Christ into her life.

Intertwined with her uplifting message is Tanya's basketball show. Frequently she calls youngsters out of the audience to help her perform. They proudly hold balls on their fingers and school pencils, and with her help learn to dribble three, then four basketballs if only for a short time.

The show moves quickly and even includes a snack for a lucky few kids.

After Tanya starts spinning a ball, she places it on a soda can and while the basketball spins around the edge, she pours the soft drink into a volunteer's mouth. Tanya offers a kindergartner an apple while juggling it with two basketballs. Each time she offers the apple, saying "Now," the child attempts a bite—until the child is doing it automatically. Then she jokingly offers the basketball instead. Invariably, the child goes for it, and the audience roars. Another young man gobbles chocolate pudding while Tanya keeps the ball spinning atop the spoon with which she's feeding him. He's delighted and afterwards scampers back to his seat with pudding and one of the posters she gives each volunteer.

After the show, she fields questions.

"Can you shoot three at a time?"

She juggles three balls and one-by-one rapidly deposits them in the basket.

"Have you ever played against the Lakers?"

Tanya smiles, and says no.

"Can you spin a ball on one finger and score?"

No answer, just further demonstrations of her ability.

From NBA games with audiences of eighteen thousand to basketball clinics with retired superstar Julius Erving in Spain, Tanya remains unaffected, recalling her modest upbringing in tiny Jefferson. About as far south in South Dakota as you can get, Jefferson sports a grocery store, a gas station, a post office, and two bars for it's five hundred friendly residents.

It's not hard to describe Tanya physically: she's 5-foot-3-inches tall, weighs 130 pounds, and has short curly brown hair and sparkling brown eyes. Fresh as the outdoors. Definitely not an uptown girl who shops Macy's, Saks, Bloomingdale's, or Neiman-Marcus. She does her shopping from the pages of Scripture, laying up her treasures in heaven where the Bible says "neither moth nor rust destroys, and where thieves do not break in or steal" (Matthew 6:20). She's the embodiment of Psalms 24:4, 5: "He who has clean hands and a pure heart . . . shall receive a blessing from the Lord."

It is harder for an observer to describe what she does. But Tanya can; does it all the time in fact. She says the trick to keeping the ball on your finger is to look for the ball's south pole as it spins. "If you put your finger right where the south pole is, then the ball will stay there," she says. "You use your opposite hand to keep it going. You have to hit it soft at first but with quick hand motions. Your hand has to flip faster than the basketball so you don't slow it down. There's really no secret to it, just a lot of practice."

Right.

Descriptions fail. You have to see it to believe it. Only clichés work here. Even when you see it you can't believe it.

When a student asks her to spin a football on her finger, she complies. For autograph requests, she puts the ball atop her pen and signs. "It's not really that hard to learn to spin a ball on something else if you can spin it on your finger real well," she says. "All you have to do is transfer that spinning ball to that pen, spoon, wherever the point of contact is." Right.

Here's Tanya's own description of her performance:

> I use three basketballs. One of them is always going behind my back. Then I just do the three-basketball weave, I call it, where the basketballs do a figure eight while you are dribbling them. Spin one, juggle two, spin one, juggle two, then juggle three, go behind your back, underneath your legs, go over the top with them; do one up and then two up, then these two cross, then they hit, then they cross, then they hit; then you can go three in a circle, then go the other way; dribble three off the floor or juggle three off the floor.

Whew. She clearly enjoys what she's doing. But after playing basketball four years and graduating in 1977 from South Dakota State University in Brookings, two hours from her hometown, Tanya was undecided about her future. She returned to Jefferson and worked with her dad for a year, making deliveries and warehousing supplies for an insulation company. After a year, doors opened into the Women's Professional Basketball League (WBL) and for three seasons she played, first with the San Francisco Pioneers and then with the Iowa Cornets. Tanya scratched to make ends meet with a salary of a thousand dollars a month and a six-month contract. Unfortunately, dwindling attendance eventually meant the league's demise and so once again, with her parents' encouragement, she returned home. But she recalls a lesson she learned.

> Because of the "unfeminine" stereotype associated with women's team sports, it's caused me to think through how I dress and how I portray being a woman athlete. I really pray about that and I am careful about that. I think it's important to dress like a lady and be feminine. It doesn't take away from your competitiveness on the court. I think you can be a woman and still be a champion athlete and be competitive.

"After the WBL folded, I didn't know what God wanted me to do," she adds. "But my parents were supportive and said, 'You always have a place here.'"

Tanya sought opportunities with basketball coaches and various ministries for which she'd performed and gradually developed her program. Now she performs for over one hundred school assemblies yearly, not to mention perhaps fifty basketball camps and coaching clinics, and over thirty high school, college, and NBA half-time shows. She's also sponsored by a shoe company, a ball company, and a clothing company, for which she does personal appearances—including one in Munich, Germany, in 1988 at "the biggest sporting goods show in the world."

She receives honorariums for each appearance, plus travel expenses. She's content with that income and states, "I just depend on God to provide. I want to be a good steward of my time, talent, and treasure."

In the fall of 1988, the NBA invited her to accompany the Boston Celtics to Madrid, Spain, for the McDonald's Cup. Games were played on Friday and Sunday with a clinic in between. Tanya and Julius Erving, the famed Dr. J were the featured clinicians. Also, Tanya performed at half time of the Celtics' games against pro teams from Spain, Italy, and Yugoslavia. She was invited back the fall of 1989 to Rome to entertain at another McDonald's Cup tourney.

Michael Jordan of the Chicago Bulls calls her a class person and one of the best he's ever seen dribble a basketball. Former Philadelphia '76er Bobby Jones simply calls her unbelievable. The late Pistol Pete Maravich called her show a pure basketball high.

Pat Williams, owner and general manager of the new National Basketball Association franchise in Orlando, calls her uniquely talented. "I've never seen a performer like her. But more importantly, she has a solid, vibrant testimony for the Lord. I wish every youngster in America could see Tanya's show and hear her share her Christian faith."

Others have called her a world-class entertainer, a fantastic person, a freewheeling performer, so astounding in her ball-handling variations that she leaves the audience gasping for breath.

Sounds like a lot of glamour and success for a little farm girl from Jefferson, South Dakota.

Tanya might agree to some extent. That *is* success, but she defines her personal success differently than most.

> For me, personal success would be reacting like Christ would react both in tough situations and in happy times. The only way that I can do that is to be filled with Christ and to be reading His Word. I memorize His Scriptures. I really ask Him to make my attitude His attitude. That's something I'm constantly working on as I turn over areas of my life to Him. That kind of success is important to me.

As a youngster, she emulated the success her older brothers and sister displayed. Because of their diligence at sports and music, she knew that she'd have to work hard, too.

She still recalls the thrill as a seventh grader of finally spinning a ball successfully. "I knew when I could get the first one, the possibilities were endless," she says, adding that even now it averages twenty-five practice hours to learn a new trick.

When Tanya's older brothers Maurice and Marc were playing college football in Ohio, they'd come home on weekends and tell stories to their thirteen-year-old sister about a freshman basketball player who could do crazy tricks with a basketball. Even though that player, George Schauer, a.k.a. "Crazy George," transferred to the University of Minnesota when Ashland College head basketball coach Bill Musselman went there, his basketball reputation stretched to South Dakota.

Intrigued, little Tanya tried spinning the basketball the way her brothers described. It took her awhile, but slowly she caught on. "When Marc and Maurice would come home, I'd show them the things I had learned when they were away. They'd get pretty excited and would tell Crazy George, 'Hey, we've got this little sister that can do what you do!' I'd bug them each time they came home to show me a new trick," she said.

I never knew what it would lead to, but I always felt down deep in my heart that God would bless and reward me for all the practicing I was doing. Finally after seven years of practicing, I got to meet "Crazy George." He was so unselfish to teach me the things he was doing. I did a camp with him, and when I showed him the things I could do, he was amazed! He just loved to work with kids and his rapport with kids was unique.

People would ask me what my hobby was, and the only thing I could think of was basketball. I really think by bringing people into my life like my brothers and sister who could serve as role models, God has honored that childlike faith that I had in wanting to use my talents to somehow serve Him. My role models would inspire me and tell me about how to use my God-given talents.

Tanya's older brothers set an example for her in other areas besides sports.

I knew there had to be more to life than just playing basketball, just going to school, just being around. Even though I had experienced a lot of success athletically and in my studies, I still had a void in my life. I went to church every Sunday and to the Fellowship of Christian Athletes meetings and I really loved God, but I never had what I'd call a personal relationship with Him.

But my older brothers and my roommate Jackie, who wasn't an athlete, would witness to me. She had a relationship with Someone that I needed, too. So finally one night I got down on my knees and asked Jesus Christ to come into my life and make me a godly woman and athlete. I wanted to turn over my life and my talents and my attitudes to Him. My brothers and Jackie really knew that I needed what they had. They were sincere and real people and had a peace in their life that I wanted.

Tanya's life didn't change drastically outwardly, because basically she was a good person who had set high standards for herself. "I never wanted to drink or smoke or do drugs or have premarital sex because my parents taught us that those things were wrong and that it was important to keep high standards for ourselves. Those things wouldn't help me achieve the goals that I had set for myself."

One of Tanya's goals was to play on a high school girls basketball team, but her high school offered none. Finally when she was a junior, in 1971–72, Jefferson started a team. Tanya had worked to be ready if the opportunity came, shooting jump shots on the gravel basketball court in front of the garage while her brothers lifted weights inside, and doing ball-handling drills on the front porch and in between the living-room furniture. Give her a ball and some air space and she'd spin until her fingers bled. She embodied the words of UCLA basketball coaching legend John Wooden who once vowed, "I will prepare, and then perhaps my chance will come."

"That kind of described me waiting for the chance to play basketball," Tanya recalls. While at South Dakota State, she helped her team become the best in the state and a contender in the regionals.

Those basketball skills have taken her around the world, to Germany, Italy, Brazil, Argentina, and even behind the Iron Curtain to Hungary. She's a member of every frequent flyer program from A to Z: American Airlines to Air Zaire. Come to think of it, scratch Air Zaire. Nevertheless, with all her traveling, when asked her favorite place to visit, she says, "Home!" As her travelbank miles accumulate, she gives the tickets to family members and close friends.

"When I'm on vacation, I just want to go home—just send me home. But I love the summer with its intensity [she's on the road from June 1 to mid-August]. You've got to be 100 percent when you get to each basketball camp even though sometimes you might be physically tired or drained." At the end of the performance she might share what God has done in her life and give out business cards imprinted with a message about her faith in Christ. She passes out over ten thousand each summer. "Whoever wants one, come up and get it," she offers. By the time they see her perform they're hooked.

She says her most gratifying shows are done inside prisons while serving with the Bill Glass Evangelistic Prison Ministry. "The first time I went into a prison I didn't know how they'd respond to what I had to offer. I was scared and I just wanted them to like me. They responded to the talent and testimony in a very positive way.

"Sometimes you see God change hearts right before your eyes. It's humbling to see them make a genuine commitment to the Lord."

Juggling four basketballs was her toughest accomplishment, she says "because you have to learn to hold four basketballs! To be able to juggle four you have to be able to hold four, and getting that was hard. With something like that you can't get instant results. Too many times today we have a fast-food mentality

where we want something now and we want it done our way."
The biggest challenge was to learn to do everything equally as
well with her weaker left hand as with her stronger right hand.
However, her greatest satisfaction comes from sharing Jesus
Christ. Her goal is Matthew 6:33 (NKJV), "Seek first the kingdom
of God. . . ."

When complimented, she receives praise humbly. "I guess in
my heart I know why I'm performing. I'm doing it to glorify
Christ, and I just say a simple thank you and make the person feel
good about complimenting me. Then I direct the praise toward
why I'm doing it. Growing up on a farm and not losing track of
my roots has really helped keep things in perspective."

She shares with others how a little farm girl who wasn't that tall
or that fast could use a simple talent to serve Him with her life.

God can use any of our talents—He gave them to us in the first place.
The most important thing was that I loved God and somehow wanted
to use my talents for Him. God can use any talent we have as long as
we're faithful to Him, as long as we set the proper goals mentally,
physically, and spiritually. God will keep expanding our opportunities
as we keep turning things over in our life and allow Him to guide and
direct us.

Out of everything I've done and every place I've gone, I've never
experienced more joy than sharing Christ and seeing somebody accept Him as their personal Savior.

Finally, Tanya sums up her philosophy with a Bible verse:
"Whatever you do in word or deed, do all in the name of the
Lord Jesus, giving thanks through Him to God the Father"
(Colossians 3:17).

# 6 *Jenna Johnson*

## Caught in the waves

OLYMPIC SWIMMER JENNA JOHNSON pulled herself from the pool at the University of Texas natatorium. The Stanford University coed quickly surveyed her opponents, inhaled deeply, and bounded onto the cold metal starting blocks. The rough, wet, sandpaper surface was comfortingly familiar.

Thousands of times before she had gone through the same routine—adjust the suit, fix the goggles, shake out the jitters. Try to get comfortable. But this time she faced added pressure. These were the 1988 Olympic Trials and Jenna, a five-time National Collegiate Athletic Association champion in the butterfly and freestyle sprints, was trying to regain a spot on the United States Olympic swim team.

Yet this time those jitters just wouldn't disappear.

Just four years earlier, sixteen-year-old Jenna had breezed through these same tryouts in Indianapolis. Then, the high school sophomore's swimming potential seemed to lie ahead a few years, possibly in the XXIV Olympiad in Seoul, Korea. Now that time had arrived and the pressure was on. Meeting the qualifying times here was one thing. But making it into the finals and the top eight, and then finishing first or second to earn a roster spot was quite another.

Jenna was born September 11, 1967, in Santa Rosa, California, just north of San Francisco up Highway 101. In 1983 she had moved to La Habra in the Los Angeles area with her mother when her parents' marriage crumbled. While "going south" might mean misfortune to some, it was a boost for Jenna's swimming career.

The family's breakup had been difficult for Jenna. Younger brothers Joel and Jacob moved in with their father, Johnnie, a basketball coach, and Jenna remained with her mother, Sharon. But she also kept close to her dad, who had encouraged her to get started with swimming. A former basketball player and one-time high school swimmer, Johnnie Johnson guided his daughter's swimming career with sound advice when she first started competing at age eight.

Once, when she'd visited a third-grade friend's house, young Jenna had been fascinated by her pal's roomful of ribbons, medals, and trophies. Curiosity piqued, she had inquired, "Where did you get all this stuff?" Her friend had explained about the local swim team, and Jenna had vowed, "I'm going to get myself some of these!"

Jenna achieved success quickly, eventually overshadowing her childhood friend. By age twelve she had begun competing year-round. Her parents and coaches appreciated her potential and encouraged her. Looking back she says,

> My parents gave me the right kind of support when I was getting started—not pushing, just encouraging me to go to practice, so it wasn't like I went because I *had* to. That made it so the motivation came from me and not from what my parents wanted me to do. That was a key, although I didn't know it at the time. Now I see a lot of kids that got pushed and they're sick of swimming. It takes so much time anyway that you can get sick just doing it.

Jenna got herself to daily practice by riding her bike to the bus stop, then taking the bus five miles to the pool. "I don't know if all kids can do that," she says now. "I think there are just some kids that have a drive in them to excel and I was like that. Like I wanted to get A's in school and I wanted to do the best in swimming I could."

Her father honed her innate skills, teaching her about natural talent versus working hard. All the athletes in the world, he would say, have one of two types of engines: either a Porsche or a Volkswagen bug. The Porsches are naturally fast and they don't have to work as hard. The VWs really have to work hard, but sooner or later they can pass up the Porsches if the Porsches don't keep themselves in shape. Ironically, this philosophy would later haunt Jenna.

> When my dad first told me that analogy, I always thought I was the VW because I was always looking at people that I wanted to be as

good as and beat someday. It was sort of like swimming was my sport. When I started learning all the strokes I realized I had the type of body that was good for swimming.

Now I look at myself as kind of the Porsche engine. But I've also worked really hard—I'm not saying I didn't work hard before, but I beat a lot of people earlier simply because I was tall. I think I was blessed with a lot of talent in the beginning, but I didn't even have to know how to do all the strokes since I could take advantage of my height.

One reason Jenna remained close to her dad was that she could always talk to him easily. "I always valued that because I knew a lot of my friends didn't have that friendship or such a great relationship with their parents even though they lived with both of them."

So it was with mixed emotions that Jenna moved to Southern California in 1983. Adjusting to a new school and family situation might be hard, but competing for the elite Industry Hills club team and working under head coach Ed Spencer would be beneficial in terms of her swimming career. And working out strenuously provided a good antidote to a trying home life and loneliness.

Her six-foot-two-inch height is advantageous in the water, but as a youngster Jenna had to face teasing from her classmates for being different—even more for her luxurious long red hair than her height. By the time she was fourteen she was six feet tall. "Yeah, I was called 'carrot top' and 'big red,' and 'daddy long legs' or 'mama long legs.' Some kids were kind of cruel to me for having red hair, but I was teased more for that than being tall." Swimming success increased her confidence and self-esteem, though she remained somewhat shy.

Her success brought attention, and the coaches in volleyball and basketball tried to recruit her for their sports. But in basketball, her glasses would go flying all over the court, and in her only track meet she "sort of tripped all over myself and couldn't even get started." So she turned down other offers, saying she "was sort of into swimming."

Jenna guarded her accomplishments from her new peers at Whittier Christian High School. By this time she was progressing from local levels to elite meets, facing ever-increasing competition.

I didn't want people to think I was bragging. Plus, I was really, really shy. I went overboard on the other side so people wouldn't think I was bragging. I didn't go into the full-on thing where, "Yeah, I'm really seriously training and thinking about going to the Olympics." I just thought it wasn't necessary. But they still asked a million questions.

One of the curious was her math teacher, Miss Turner. An avid sports fan, Miss Turner inquired, "How much 'into' swimming are you?"

Jenna opened up and described her practice schedule.

"You really *do* swim a lot! Where are you ranked and where are your meets and what kind do you go to?" Casual interest deepened into enthusiastic support and Miss Turner faithfully attended Jenna's meets. Always the following Monday morning she would announce to the entire class how Jenna had done, embarrassing the young athlete.

"When I changed high schools it was really hard because I didn't know anybody, not a single person at the school. So I spent a couple of weeks eating lunch alone. I felt really stupid, but then a couple of girls reached out to me and we ended up being really good friends." Bolstered by their kindness, Jenna became more comfortable at the new high school—as well as in the water.

Jenna's times in the freestyle and butterfly sprints ranked her in the top ten nationally. She labored diligently and as she says, "I never really talked much in practice. I went to practice to work hard. It was fun, but it wasn't like I talked that much or joked around. I've loosened up some now."

Now her thoughts turned toward making the Olympic team.

I knew I was in the general area where I might make it, but I knew the competition was really fierce, too. People would come up to me when I first went to Whittier Christian and say, "Oh, you'll make the team." But I wasn't sure they realized how hard it was to make it. A lot of people are unaware of sports, especially swimming, because it's not covered very much except for the big meets like the Olympics. I thought I was a long shot—maybe in '88. But it seemed unlikely '84 would be my year.

It had all seemed so easy then. No pressure. Nothing to lose. Jenna even used to tell herself, "If I make it, that's great. If I don't there's '88."

The underdog role suited the young pup to a T. As in Mary T. The great Mary T. Meagher, rival and world record holder in Jenna's events and the favorite to win the Olympic gold medal.

To help Jenna prepare for the Olympic Trials in 1984, the teachers at Whittier Christian High School had given the high school sophomore the last week off from school and finals. They knew she was nervous, and the added pressure of preparing for finals could have detracted from her preparations for the Olympic Trials.

"You're getting A's in all your classes anyway," offered Miss Turner. "We want you to rest and prepare for Indianapolis."

Jenna was thrilled.

The teachers supported her in other ways, too, chipping in for a letterman's jacket from the school since Whittier Christian had no school-sponsored swim team. She might make the Olympic team, but she could never make the WCHS team since it had none.

Coach Ed Spencer tried to alleviate some pressure, too, emphasizing optimistically, "You only have to finish in the top six to go, Jenna, because that's how many they take for the relay. It would be really good if you could make it in the 100-meter freestyle so the pressure would be off during your butterfly. I really think that's your best chance, but why risk it?" he pointed out.

Jenna swam smoothly in that first event, stroking to a third-place finish with a time of 56.20, guaranteeing a slot on the 1984 team as a relay member and barely missing out on the chance to swim in the individual event. Two days later came the 100-meter butterfly. Jenna, still pumped, beat world-record-holder Mary T. Meagher in the event! Through 1989, Jenna's time (59.08) remained the third best time ever worldwide.

She would be going back to L.A. as an Olympian! Jenna, at sixteen, was one of the two youngest swimmers, male or female, to represent the U.S. in the XXIII Games. She was such a wide-eyed newcomer that she carefully studied her new teammates' events and learned their names. "For instance, I looked up to Mary T. a lot, but at the Olympics I could barely talk to her because I was scared to."

"I was really excited and everyone was so nice. I didn't even know half the world record holders' names—I was clueless. I got on an elevator with [world champion high hurdler] Edwin Moses and I knew who he was, but I'm sure he didn't even notice that I was there! I couldn't believe we were on the same Olympic team representing our country!"

Jenna earned three medals: a gold medal in the 4-X-100-meter freestyle relay, a silver behind the legendary Mary T. in the 100-meter butterfly, and a gold in the 4-X-100-meter medley relay. Although Mary T. had replaced her position in the butterfly leg during the finals, Jenna's swim in the morning preliminaries had helped the medley relay qualify in first place for the finals that night.

Jenna followed up her Olympic success by chalking up two NCAA titles in the 50-yard freestyle, two in the 100-yard freestyle, and one in the 100-yard butterfly. As a freshman at the 1986 NCAAs she was the top individual scorer with 77 points, winning three individual titles (the 50-freestyle, 100-freestyle, and 100-butterfly), placing second in the 200-freestyle, and swimming two winning relay stints. That excellent performance earned her the 1986 Broderick Award for swimming, an NCAA award recognizing the top athlete in each sport for excellence in athletics, academics, and leadership.

But all that was old news. There's an adage in sports that you're only as good as your last race. Yesterday's news fades faster than a falling star. News clippings about swimming stars get soggy pretty fast.

Now it was 1988. Now Jenna was the favorite. She was no longer the under pup, but the top dog.

This time it was different. Instead of having everything to win, she had everything to lose. People expected her to win. Now pressure was trying to gain a victim.

Her Porsche engine had been running smoothly, or so it seemed. "I remember feeling so much better in '84 and '86," she recalls. "In 1988 I never felt that great in the water. Maybe my body was different. And I kept comparing all the time.

"When I was sixteen I was really skinny, *really* skinny—only 145 pounds. Later I was so much stronger, even though I weighed 165. I had more muscle and everything. But negative thoughts kept coming into my head, like, 'If I weighed twenty pounds less I'd be much faster.'"

Prior to college, Jenna had eaten whatever she wanted. "I never used to think about it. And I could eat what I wanted whenever I was hungry because I had such a high metabolism." But Jenna's body was changing. Added weight meant more bulk to pull through the water. "I was kind of a late bloomer and in college my body started filling out. I had to think more about watching my food intake."

But with the pressures of living up to being an Olympic medalist and maintaining her scholarship at academically rigorous Stanford, Jenna found herself eating to help overcome depression. Nibbling to help the nerves. "It seemed like the more people talked about it, the more I worried and the worse it got. Every year I'd gain a little more," she said.

> If you saw me walking down the street you wouldn't say, "Man, she needs to lose weight!" But to be a swimmer you have to be pretty thin. And I'd never had to worry about that. Maybe other girls, but not me.
>
> Our whole family is pretty skinny and my dad kept teasing me, "Jenna you'd better watch out!" And I felt kind of yucky about myself because I wasn't this skinny little thing. I was self-conscious. It's the nature of this sport—with everyone in swimsuits, the first thing you notice when you see someone you haven't seen in a while is whether they've gained or lost weight. It's really bad. And your opponents use that to psyche themselves up to beat you.

Pressure dulled her senses as Jenna gamely climbed onto the starting blocks at the University of Texas. Her mind raced between fear and euphoria. She had been sluggish during warmups, but the twenty-year old badly wanted to once again compete for the opportunity of representing the United States.

"Oh, I just want to make this team so bad," the thoughts rocked and rolled through her head like waves on the ocean. But she couldn't help also thinking how awful it would be to *not* make the Olympic team again. And this race, the 100-meter freestyle, was her best chance.

The starter called the swimmers into position. "Take your marks . . ." The horn blared, sending eight sleek and talented swimmers into the water. She struggled to the finish. After all the heats were over, Jenna—NCAA champion, Broderick award winner, and Olympic medalist—hadn't even made the finals! "It was unbelievable. Like, 'How could I go this slow?' I never swam that slow in a big meet before.

"It's hard sometimes to let a bad swim bounce off you and go on to the next race and do well. I have trouble with that sometimes; well, most of the time. I was telling myself, 'That's okay. The butterfly is a different stroke. Two more days of rest and you'll be ready.'" Jenna was telling that to herself, but her inner self wasn't listening very well.

She swam terribly in the 100-meter butterfly. She started out okay, but lagging at the end, barely finished the race. "I was thinking, 'What's going on here?' It's not like I didn't train or anything. I worked just as hard, if not harder. I don't know what happened." Perhaps the previously fine-tuned Porsche engine was out of sync.

Because the 50-meter freestyle had been added this year, there would be another opportunity for Jenna. "But when we got to the pool I just wasn't into it at all. I was just up there thinking, 'Why am I even here?' It was really an emotional time for me." Jenna's dad tried to console her by telling her to relax and quit worrying. But nothing seemed to help. Pressure, the enemy, was about to claim a victim.

During that time Jenna retreated privately to her diary, daring to express on paper what she couldn't face publicly. "I wrote so much that week. It helps me to get things out when I write them down. But then it kind of made me dwell on it too much. If you're playing on the wrong track, it makes you concentrate more on what's going wrong.

"After I figured out this meet wasn't going to be a good meet for me, I feel I took it pretty well." Outwardly she put on a brave face, even smiling when people looked at her. "I knew they were thinking, 'She's hurt, she must be bummed. The worst thing that could happen to somebody would be to not make the Olympic team.' I needed to rely on God a lot for strength."

Because of her priorities as a Christian, she concluded there were a lot more things in life.

I was confused and I didn't understand why it had to be this way, but I knew there had to be a reason. I had prayed so hard for so long that whatever happened would be God's will. I didn't even think of not being in Seoul that summer, and didn't have any other plans because I didn't think I *wouldn't* be in Seoul. I made a special effort to smile at others because I wanted to show them that I wasn't going to go around moping.

If I wasn't a Christian, I think I would have fallen apart. When you do something for so long your identity can be totally wrapped up in that. Like, "There's Jenna-the-swimmer." And I'm known as a swimmer. If swimming was the main thing in my life and I didn't have God, then when I failed at swimming, I'd be a failure as a person, too.

But when you have God, you know that He loves you and gave you this talent in the first place to glorify Him. And if it's His will that you do well with it, and if you're willing to put in the work, and if you're putting Him first, then "God causes all things to work together for good who love God, to those who are called according to His purpose" (Romans 8:28).

When Jenna returned to California, she allowed herself a little adjustment time in private at home, but when she was out, she determined to act like "this is the way it's going to be and this is the way it's supposed to be." But finally, when September came, so did the difficult reality. Jenna was Seoul'd out. "When I was watching the Olympics on TV, I couldn't believe I was watching them and wasn't there. I didn't like watching them and not being there. I still don't quite understand what happened."

The college junior-to-be checked with other prominent coaches regarding what she might have done wrong in her training. "The thing that bothered me most was people kept putting emphasis on my weight and I started getting really paranoid about it. I had a lot of friends that were bulimic and a lot of them were swimmers."

Jenna describes a girl she knew who was a private junk food eater.

> She'd eat junk out of the candy bar machines in the dorm. She'd put the wrappers someplace where she thought we wouldn't find them. We'd find them and wonder when she ate them. Later on we started wondering about her, and she admitted she had a problem. She never had a problem with throwing up; she just ate until she felt gross and then she would quit eating for a long time.

Weekly, then triweekly weigh-ins at Stanford added to the swimmers' pressure. "We'd do crazy things like run the night before the weigh-in so we'd weigh less. And starve ourselves and stuff like that. I was falling into that stuff [anorexia/bulimia] gradually." Jenna described her feelings to a friend who'd been bulimic as a child. She warned Jenna, "You better watch out because it looks like you're heading that way." Jenna hated that this was happening. "It was becoming an obsession," she recalls.

Jenna recovered from her 1988 Olympic-year disappointments to post great times in her 1989 NCAA events, winning the 100-yard butterfly as Stanford took the NCAA team title, and placing second in the 100-yard freestyle. It was a fitting finish to a stellar collegiate career that yearly saw Stanford place in the top three as Jenna broke numerous NCAA and American records in her events. She was called the greatest women's swimmer in Stanford history by the Stanford media guide.

The leading scorer at the 1988 Pac-10 meet, the Stanford co-captain won many other honors during those four years: qualifying for the Pan-Pacific Championships after placing second in the U.S. Long Course Nationals, winning gold (400-meter freestyle relay team), silver (100-meter freestyle), and bronze (100-meter butterfly); and representing the United States at the 1986 World Championships in Madrid, finishing second in the 100-meter freestyle, fourth in the 50-meter freestyle, and fifth in the 100-meter freestyle. She also helped the 400-meter freestyle and 400-meter medley relay teams to second-place finishes.

Her 1989 comeback was a satisfying personal triumph. Following her collegiate season, Jenna entered the Long Course Nationals at the McDonald's Swim Stadium on the University of Southern California campus, site of the 1984 Olympics. She realized her past glory by forgetting past disappointments and pressing on. Jenna tied for second in the 100-meter butterfly, making the national team bound for Tokyo and the Pan-Pacific Championships and for the U.S./USSR dual meet later—the Alamo Cup in Atlanta. Her teammates elected her co-captain. In Tokyo, she finished third behind two Chinese women in the individual event (1:01.01), while the medley relay team with Jenna swimming the butterfly won the gold medal. In Atlanta, Jenna won her event with a 1:01.65, as the American women beat the Soviets, 87–43.

Her comeback complete, Jenna retired, hoping to pursue a career in communications—broadcasting, writing, or public speaking—when she finished her degree at Stanford. Having attained her academic goal while also working hard to maximize her swimming talent properly had paid handsome benefits. She was the Volkswagen bug with the Porsche engine.

"This past year I almost got my weight down to where I was my freshman year when I swam. It was good for my swim times."

And for her self-esteem.

"The time I've invested in swimming has been very much worth it, even though I haven't gotten to do some things other normal kids do."

Jenna concludes, "There are so many good things I've gotten from swimming. Through swimming I learned to set goals and focus on fulfilling them. A lot of people don't do that or don't know how to. I'll carry that ability with me the rest of my life."

# 7

# *Kirsten Hanssen Ames*

## In His steps

IN THE HIGH-POWERED ATHLETIC arena, national champion triathlete Kirsten Hanssen Ames is noble in both victory and defeat, reminding one of eras when sporting competition somehow was thought to build character, not reveal it. She graciously thanks God for her abilities and for providing her with the strength and endurance to compete. She clearly enjoys her relationship with the Lord—as well as triathlon competition, which includes swimming, biking, and running.

Kirsten races with a certain aggressive style and grace—others have said nothing short of a brick wall will stop her. She'll compete to the maximum, then turn and hug her nearest rival. She wants to be competitive but not combative. She is greatly respected within triathlon for this attitude.

Kirsten believes she can be feminine as well as strong. Both qualities impressed businessman/triathlete Robert Ames and he wanted to get to know her.

She, in turn, was impressed by his neatness, promptness, and the way he treated his friends. "They were important to him. He would put down anything for his friends," she says. "I also saw the faith he had in God and how it was important to him to read his Bible daily. I can't believe God saved someone like that for me!" Robert, a 5-foot-10-inch sandy blond, is also an expert skier and an examiner for the Professional Ski Instructors of America.

On Easter Sunday, 1989, atop Colorado's spectacular Mount Quandary, Robert proved he was in no quandary about their future together when he got down on his knees and romantically proposed.

Married November 11, 1989, in Wichita, Kansas, Kirsten and Robert are making their home in Steamboat Springs, Colorado, where he is the director of marketing and advertising for a large specialty ski retail chain. A quaint village in the summer, Steamboat's population swells to twenty thousand during ski season. Despite increased training difficulties with no indoor pool or the fantastic facilities she had in Denver, Kirsten remains unperturbed. She doesn't feel cheated but challenged.

"They keep the water heated outdoors in the winter and I might have to wear a wetsuit," she says almost matter-of-factly, as though that's the way everyone should swim. Then she adds almost as an afterthought, "But I still get chilled." That's vintage Kirsten, admitting the problem but seeing the positive. "I have good support from Robert and I want to do quality events, even the longer events like the Ironman." She plans on racing for at least a few more years, as well as coaching at triathlon training camps.

"I definitely wanted 'Ames' on my name. I don't need to stick to just myself. Robert is an important part of me," Kirsten says. They enjoy skate-skiing and biking together, and hanging around the kitchen. But they have to take turns wearing the chef's apron.

"He's a great cook and I'm a great eater!" Kirsten laughs. Robert is renowned for his pumpkin cheesecake, which he often gives as birthday treats, and his chicken dishes and pasta dishes (including clam linguini), and for fabulous popovers.

Once called the Sandra Dee of triathlon, Kirsten is a bouncy, friendly, energetic, wholesome girl-next-door type with sparkling blue-green eyes and blonde hair. There's no such word as *boring* in her pocket dictionary. Having grown up in Wichita, Kansas, an only child, she can always find a way to entertain herself, even if it's just whistling while she works or, even better, singing hymns while she plays. She is to triathlon what Orel Hershiser is to baseball: a bonafide superstar and determined competitor with a deep faith in God. But if his nickname is "the Bulldog" hers would have to be "the Beagle."

Born in San Diego, Kirsten soon moved with her parents, Susie and Gary (who had met and courted at the University of Colorado), to Boulder. When she was ten her father, an executive with Beech Aircraft, transferred to Wichita. For Mrs. Hanssen, the Great Plains seemed more plain than great after living in the mountains and pines, and building relationships took time. Yet the move brought the Hanssens into contact with a family who encouraged them to join them in attending church and got Kirsten involved on a swim team with their triplets Reed, Brad, and Anne.

"With triplets, it seems like one is always getting left out, but it didn't seem to matter to Anne if she was that one. Anne was only ten but she had a deep friendship with Jesus Christ. She would share verses and be excited about the Bible and she had an unusual love for the Lord at an early age. Her best friend always seemed to be Jesus no matter what happened with pairing up or being left out or whatever," Kirsten says.

Kirsten, puzzled that a friend could know God in such a personal way, kept observing Anne until she, too, wanted to place her trust in Jesus Christ. "I just realized I wanted that same consistent friend in Jesus that Anne had. But finally I knew that Jesus died for my sin, that He forgave me, and that He's given me an eternal home in heaven."

Within a few years of moving to Wichita, Kirsten, Susie, and Gary had all accepted the Lord through the influence of this loving family.

Kirsten's parents taught her from childhood to see the positive side of disappointments—to look for the best in any situation. They taught her to entertain herself and, whenever possible, to enjoy being around friends.

Triathlon embodies both elements: training long distances alone and yet also working in groups. An individual must be inwardly motivated to excel but group encouragement is readily available. Kirsten integrates both. Her parents' teaching is highly valuable, yet it's been her personal relationship with God that has brought lasting fulfillment.

"My parents encouraged me when I was young to be involved in Christian activities and Bible studies with our church youth group," she says, describing how she participated in a singing group of three hundred kids that performed in large Wichita concert halls. "I learned there that my life is not based on how I perform but on identifying with God. My goal is not to be successful but to be faithful."

Her parents, she says, tried to help her learn to trust the Lord and to realize that things are going to work out for our good when we trust in God and are called according to His purpose. "Even though the small things can really add up, God has blessed me with a spirit that goes on and doesn't take a hurt or disappointment real hard."

Meanwhile, in the water, Kirsten's times ranked her as high as fourth in her age group nationally in the 100-yard breaststroke and qualified her at age fourteen for the Junior Olympics in the 400-meter individual medley. Entering high school, she wanted to be involved in more extracurricular activities, so she swam for Wichita Southeast High only during the short two-month high school season and participated in music and drama ventures the rest of the time. She turned down swimming athletic scholarships, too. Nevertheless, the swimming discipline prepared her well for triathlon and she notes the benefits today.

Since most triathletes have running backgrounds, they must learn to swim in the open water. "Swimming efficiency is about 85 percent technique, and if you come from a swimming background it's helpful, since you'll never be as absolutely frightened of the water conditions we encounter." Despite her past success, she says ironically, that swimming is now about her weakest event. "Some of the women triathletes who continued competitive swimming through college are still very strong in that event," she says, "but I enjoyed my break."

It's true that triathlon is not every man's sport. Or every woman's for that matter. From the unusual few who, bored with simple marathons, started the sport in the early 1970s, to growing legions numbering into the hundred thousands, it's still the ultimate self-challenge: Can I do it?

For Kirsten, it's competing for a higher goal and an inner satisfaction. She says that attitude comes from the hours she spends talking with God when she's running, swimming, and biking, and the time she spends reading the Bible. Whether on stage or in magazine articles, she exhorts young athletes and consistently and humbly credits God for her success. An enthusiastic speaker, she received a rousing ovation after challenging an audience at a Colorado women's sports festival to look to God.

"All triathletes get asked why they do this sport," she says, remarking that the sport's great demands and the individual's high expectations tend to cause burn-out. It actually may be more like brown-out—a lowering of competitive desire. Yet Kirsten remains challenged even after competing for five years, for her inspiration comes from beyond herself.

I'm racing and training to glorify God. My foundation is completely based on my relationship with Jesus Christ. He gives me talents and strengths and motivates me to keep working out. And I love being out-of-doors in God's creation, talking with God, and taking time to pray for friends and their needs.

There's so much hope when God is in control. Even though there are losses and sometimes things go wrong—a poor transition or a flat tire—to put it in God's perspective, there might be other reasons, like how God is shaping your character and willpower. You have to be able to see beyond yourself. And even though my performance might be down I still might be able to share my faith with someone and let them know how much I love Jesus, and that's very rewarding. I want to do my best each moment and use my athletic ability to glorify God. Knowing that I've done that is much more of a reward than the temporary rewards of a trophy or prize money.

Indeed, the sport's reputation is epitomized by a 1982 Hawaii Ironman Triathlon incident recorded on ABC-TV's "Wide World of Sports." The leading female competitor collapsed yards from the finish line and while she crawled to the end, was dramatically passed, finishing second. So-called international distances, or the newly-termed Olympic distances, are not so grueling. Now standardized, the distances include a one-mile swim, 25-mile bike ride, and 6-mile run.

Sometimes in a triathlon you conquer the beast inside, and sometimes it conquers you. The triathletes face that challenge within and without in the America's Paradise Triathlon. "The Beast" is actually the most printable description of a particularly steep course section. Other descriptions range "from the slime (definitely not the sublime) to the ridiculous."

It's 7:00 A.M. on the slumbering Caribbean island of Saint Croix. The tropical island awakens with the starter's pistol for the 1989 America's Paradise Triathlon. A brisk, nearly two-mile ocean swim precedes a 59-mile bike ride and a 20-kilometer (12-mile) run. Only the best in the world-class women's field, including defending champion Kirsten, will finish before noon.

The rain forest's shade welcomes competitors after the transition from swimming to bicycling. Nevertheless, at the halfway point—mile 32—looms "the Beast," an unforgiving uphill ribbon of asphalt built specifically to challenge the world's best triathletes.

Cycling uphill is like running up a "black diamond" ski slope, and nearly impossible for all but the most intrepid. Choose the wrong gear and gravity takes effect—you can't progress and you'll find it's a painfully slow walk to the top. Choose the right gear and still your thighs and lungs will be screaming for oxygen. It's seven minutes of sheer agony for that half mile. Many competitors will choose simply to walk their bikes up rather than risk breaking concentration or possible injury in dismounting alone.

The Beast's unimaginable and nearly insurmountable 27 percent grade (the asphalt road, so steep it had to be built from the top down, provides additional access to an isolated resort) prevented all but three women pros from conquering it. One who triumphed was diminutive Kirsten Hanssen, who once again showed it's not your physical size but the size of your heart. Because of that kind of supreme effort, television commentators call her the most deceptively strong woman in triathlon competition. And she is. She could be a walking advertisement for Reynold's aluminum foil: strong yet light.

With high-tech, upswept V-shaped handlebars and teardrop-shaped racing helmet, Kirsten knows the right equipment can mean the difference between victory and defeat. Following pre-race practice rides, she's carefully tuned her bike and after being seventeenth out of the water, she picks up twelve places, knocking off eight competitors while climbing the Beast and passing another two in the last transition. Finally, she works the kinks out of her running stride and, cheered on by 35,000 spectators, finishes second, in 4 hours and 53 minutes. Later she credits her runner-up finish to persevering up the Beast.

As a first-year pro in 1986, Kirsten won three U.S. Triathlon Series titles and the Coke Grand Prix number one ranking—all the more impressive considering she was punching the clock full time in Denver as a computer programmer. Monday mornings meant running her fingers over a keyboard, not running her legs around the block. She planned her workouts around lunch breaks and free time.

In 1987 she quit her job and went pro full time, taking seven USTS titles (including two in one weekend—one on Saturday in Atlanta and one on Sunday in Columbus, Ohio) plus the top grand prix ranking, and being selected female Triathlete of the Year. Of the twenty-two events she entered, she won sixteen and finished second in four others. And in 1988 she added four more USTS triumphs despite a late-season wrist injury.

Kirsten clearly enjoys what she's doing. The self-named "jolly jogger" of college days has become one of the sport's elite. Her outer strength is quickly apparent: at 5 feet, 3 inches and 103 pounds she has only 8½ percent body fat. In comparison, a typical twenty-eight-year-old female would have over 20 percent body fat. Kirsten says her body fat percentage is an estimation, because "the charts didn't go down low enough." There may be room for JELL-O, as they say, but not for the jiggles on this trim body. In 1988 triathlon insiders considered her, after four years in the sport, the fittest U.S. female triathlete. Kirsten credits her hard work and her faith in God for that. Yet it's her inner strength which carries her through.

"You can't jump in there all at once and start competing in triathlons. I had to build my endurance. There's discipline in workouts, in going ahead and training even though you might be fatigued," she notes, drawing a comparison between the Christian life and a marathon.

Running a marathon is like life: just a step-by-step, decision-by-decision, day-by-day task of pressing on. When you're preparing for the Ironman you have to run all those miles and yet you know it's going to pay off when you're able to finish the race. There's discipline in the Christian life, too. You have to make consistent choices to do what Christ would have you to do and trust God for His rewards.

While a University of Colorado coed, she began jogging around "Greektown" with her Kappa Alpha Theta sorority sisters. Dorm life, institutional food, studying, and college blahs were something to be reckoned with and, she says,

I found I performed my daily tasks better when I was running and working out, and I was so encouraged by others' compliments. I've heard Mom mention many times that we have so many more opportunities as women in sports today; that a woman involved in athletics is so much more respected now.

Fitness makes a woman look good. It's beautiful that a woman can be athletic *and* feminine. Man and woman were created different physically and with different capabilities. It's important for the woman to uphold her feminine role and not try to be a man.

Kirsten attributes her athletic ability to her mom, who she says enjoys an active but not competitive lifestyle of swimming and biking.

While competing in one Denver road race, Kirsten met an older age-group runner who, impressed that she could maintain his pace, encouraged her to seek out a local track club. As they ran and talked he shared technical information and told her she had great potential. Little did he realize how prophetic he was. But Kirsten still doesn't consider herself primarily a runner.

Kirsten's high grade point average as a student (in 1984, she graduated magna cum laude with a Business degree in information systems) might lead one to infer that she was a book jock or Library Lilly, but having fun was just as important to her. Her parents had said their college years were the most fun years of their lives and Kirsten wanted her experience to be similar. She also attended Bible studies and got involved with Campus Crusade for Christ. She even forsook a potential collegiate swimming scholarship because she wanted to do more than swim, eat, study, then swim, swim, swim. Making the swim team just didn't seem adventurous enough.

But when the student newspaper ran an ad seeking people with pizazz, she hoped they were looking for her. She enthusiastically tried out as a dance line girl with the CU marching band and made the squad. Those high steps would be a tuneup for bigger things.

While at CU she ran in her first road race with some sorority sisters and placed in the top 10 percent. That entree led the way to more races, so in 1984 when her father mentioned one summer weekend that he was going to do a triathlon, he invited her to enter, too. She won that women's short-course event in Wichita in a forty-minute lark. Within two-and-a-half years, that casual interest became a full-time occupation as she quickly graduated to longer distances.

To complete international-length triathlons you don't have to be faster than a locomotive. Or more powerful than a speeding bullet. Or able to leap tall buildings at a single bound. Or wear a caped red and blue costume with a big letter S on the chest. All that might help, of course (cape and tights optional), but it's not requisite. For in the spirit of the Olympic code, "Not the winning but the taking part," triathletes attempt to improve their own levels of endurance. There are unlimited age-group categories and Kirsten voices appreciation for the competitive efforts of "the masters." For triathletes, races are not so much against others as against themselves.

To finish the course takes unwavering fortitude and infinite determination. Kirsten draws hers from her deep faith in God. She's competing not to please herself, she says, but to honor the Lord.

She's racing to win more than trophies and prize money, although as a professional she recognizes their importance. "I'm racing for imperishable crowns that can't be exchanged for anything else. Finishing in first place is wonderful, but even better is that in my acceptance speech I can give the glory to God and say that He was my strength in competition."

Dangers abound in each triathlon leg: precarious, sometimes frigid open-water swims; biking while battling cars on city streets; and maintaining fluid-levels while running up-to-marathon distances. However, even regular daily training can present hazards. Kirsten attests to that.

In August of 1988, while training two months prior to her first-ever Hawaii Ironman Triathlon, a car turned abruptly in front of her speeding bike. Braking hard, Kirsten launched herself over the bike's handlebars, missing the car but hitting the pavement hard and breaking her wrist. Undaunted, she trained on, left wrist encased in a bright blue fiberglass cast. The cast is visible in the collector's card picture of Kirsten (cycling hunched over her bike's handlebars and wearing hot pink bike shorts and tank top) that appeared in *Sports Illustrated for Kids*. Seemingly unaffected by the injury, she says she just had to live with a soggy arm for a while.

Ironman distances are awesome: a 2.4-mile ocean swim, a 112-mile bike ride, a 26.2-mile run (marathon). Even with the cast, Kirsten completed the Ironman, setting an American women's record of 9 hours, 37 minutes and finishing as the third woman. Like many whose dream is just to complete the event, much less place in the top 10, she, too, received immense satisfaction from the fact that her training had allowed her to finish.

Later when her cast was removed, Kirsten discovered fine Hawaiian sand still embedded inside. In 1989, even though she improved her time to 9 hours, 24 minutes she still finished third. Satisfied with lowering her time by a full thirteen minutes without the cast (or the sand), she also had learned to appreciate safety. "Every day now when I come off the bike with a safe ride I'm thankful!" she observes. "I'm really grateful for how God watches out for me when I'm out on the road so much."

More common triathlon hindrances include adverse weather or flat bicycle tires. Riders like Kirsten who train in Colorado view approaching storms knowing they might get pelted by the rain and hail, but nevertheless remain willing to challenge the elements. Kirsten seems to remain upbeat through those kinds of distractions.

Perseverance and persistence are daily things. Often you'll plan workouts and rides and the weather will change it. That's a distraction but just something you have to lift up to the Lord. It's the same way with our everyday activities—negative things may come in to distract us and we just have to persevere by trusting and seeking God.

There are days when I go out for my bike ride and get two flat tires and I wonder, "Why am I doing this?" Then if you get rained on it seems ridiculous. You can get so dirty. And yet at other times the storms just seem to float right on by as you approach.

Even with all her crowning achievements, Kirsten looks beyond the laurels, write-ups, and television interviews. "I don't see how someone can make it, either as an athlete or in their job, if they don't have purpose. There has to be something solid in your life to get you through the highs and lows. I'll always know God has made me a winner, whether I'm broken or injured, first or last, or healthy or whatever. Being able to share that through my platform in athletics means so much."

For Kirsten, that doesn't mean just when she's the champion on top of the world. She believes that sometimes God uses our defeats to teach us and to reach others. In 1988, while seeking a "three-peat," a third consecutive national championship at Hilton Head, South Carolina, she finished a disastrous nineteenth. But in a local church the next day she shared that she wasn't disappointed. She told the assemblage, "We are all winners in Christ because His love is not based on how we perform." In her message of hope she referred to 1 Corinthians 15:57, 58: "Thanks be to God, who gives us the victory through our Lord Jesus Christ. Therefore . . . be steadfast, immovable, always abounding in the work of the Lord, knowing that your toil is not in vain in the Lord."

Triumph or misfortune, Kirsten takes it all in stride. Or stroke, whichever the case may be. She'll swim from 9,000 to 16,000 meters a week (three or four days); run 40 to 50 miles a week (five or six days); and bike nearly every day—up to 350 miles a week. In other words Kirsten has gotten to know her neighborhood as well as Mr. Rogers knows his. She can probably name every pothole, dip, and dog. Nevertheless, she enjoys biking the most. "You can go farther on a bike and see so much more! After twenty minutes of running I want to turn around. But it's very important to do consistently even those things that you don't like to do. Being sporadic will not help your overall effort."

Kirsten may train from two to seven hours daily, usually doing two of the events per day and eating 4,000 to 8,000 calories. Before she turned pro full time, coworkers would be astounded at what she would put away during breaks. "People couldn't believe it. They all wanted to have my problem of trying to keep weight on!" she jokes, but adds, "It's not all it's cracked up to be to have to keep eating so that you don't lose weight and get too skinny."

The tedium of solitary training is broken up by swimming and biking with different groups of people. "It's a really freeing feeling being on my bike outside and praying for friends. I just really enjoy all the beauty in God's creation. There are times when you head out and the desire is not there, but once you do it feels great. There's lots involved with the sport."

That's an understatement.

To get to a competition you have to carefully pack and unpack your bike and its spare parts. Then you must remember swimsuit, wetsuit, cap, and goggles; bike shoes, helmet, headband, sunscreen, and possibly bike shorts; running shoes, sunglasses, headband, visor, perhaps a little snack. Whatever makes you comfortable. No wonder most triathletes are office workers with college degrees. You don't just need a uniform plus a pair of sneakers and socks. Triathletes can't be like the NBA player who appeared at a game bringing only two left shoes, creating a new statistical category: DNP/BTLS (did not play/ brought two left shoes).

She's been known to run hills with heavy shoes and to do "repeats" up and down Denver's steepest inclines, all in the name of improvement. Intervals are often added to her cycling regimen: a minute hard, a minute easy, two minutes hard, two minutes easy, three minutes hard, three minutes easy. No wonder she's Queen of the Road. Sometimes she'll bike in groups, but often she works out alone because in races there's no "drafting" (riding directly behind another biker within two bike lengths) allowed. "In triathlons that's pretty much how you race—against yourself and the clock. You have to be able to push yourself—it's just you out there."

Despite the rigors, the sport is flourishing worldwide. There's speculation that it will be a 1996 Olympic medal sport and that triathlon may be a lower-cost replacement for the not-so-modern pentathlon (competition in five military-style skills—shooting, swimming, fencing, horseback riding, and cross-country running). The pentathlon is a costly event because of the equestrian requirements and has gained fewer adherents in its eighty years than triathlon has gained in fifteen.

"I'm always looking ahead, beyond the pain and bad things that occur on the course or in my life. I can withstand a little bit of difficulty now because of the hope and joy ahead," Kirsten says, recalling the verses of Hebrews 12:1, 2 about running with endurance and keeping our eyes fixed on Jesus. "I used to do a lot of memory work when I was younger and I really should reprioritize that. Even though I'm not in church as consistently as I'd like because I travel so much, I still try to spend time with the Lord daily."

One such travel period went like this: Miami to Phoenix, back East to Tampa, back to Scottsdale, then to Atlanta, and out to California, racing each weekend. Kirsten says she has to have a foundation in her life that's consistent, a relationship with Jesus Christ.

Athletics and sports aren't going to last forever. There are going to be wins and losses, ups and downs, hard times and great ones, and there's got to be something consistent that keeps you going and can hold all that together.

I'll miss it a lot if I don't run or work out. It's good for me mentally and physically. It's good for letting off steam. Just yesterday when I was running I had to thank the Lord for the endorphins, the runner's high, setting in. It was so relaxing I could begin to forget about all the other things I had to do. And yet I don't want to run to release stress by just running when I should be taking the problems to the Lord.

When problems occur—or when everything's fine—that's when I need to turn to God. I want to tell God thanks when I'm running that He has allowed me this time to lift my problems and burdens before Christ. Jesus really has become my best friend.

# 8

# Rosie Black

## Diamond in the rough

BORIS BECKER'S TENNIS OPPONENTS have .49 of a second to return his serve. Don't blink or you'll miss it.

Try hitting softball ace Rosie Black's pitch in .27 seconds.

Don't even *think* about blinking.

Firing away from 40 feet at 100 miles per hour, it requires nearly the same reaction time as catching a twelve-inch ruler dropped from just above your fingers. On some nights, those pitches look like aspirin tablets coming in sideways.

The queen of diamonds is awesome. For most of Rosie's games, the headline for the next day is already written; "The Queen Reigns. Long Live the Queen!" The sportswriter has only to add the winning margin.

Rosie serves up a phenomenal sixteen different pitches at various speeds (Take that Orel Hershiser and Dwight Gooden!)—an assortment of rises, in-rises, straight drops, off-speed drops, sinking curves, flat curves, knuckleballs, and three or four backbreaking changeups. She'll throw strikes from between her legs, from behind her back, from second base, from her knees, with double pumps, and while blindfolded. The heat from her fastball could launch a rocket.

And this summer she's appearing on softball diamonds near you. Rosie travels the globe performing with her coed four-player softball club, the Queen and Her Court. Matched nightly against male nine-player squads, Rosie wins 96 percent of her games while pitching up to 150 games each summer. Rosie rolls up what major leaguers would call "career year" statistics each season. In 1989, Rosie, who turned thirty-eight in 1990, pitched 80 and lost only two. Every year since she made her debut at age thirteen with the first appearance of the Queen and Her Court, the most frequently asked questions are "Why are you doing this?" and "How much longer are you going to play?" Rosie says she plays for more than game challenges. Prior to each game, she takes a microphone and shares a short gospel message of God's love and forgiveness.

"We have a number of different goals that we're trying to achieve when we go out there," the winningest-ever women's softball pitcher says. "My number one goal is my ministry. I want to play for God and do my best for Him and His glory. As I share simply before the game about my faith in God, some people hear who would never go to church and might never get to hear the gospel." Rosie considers herself a seed-planter as she carefully explains God's love through Jesus Christ. She personally answers letters, often sending Bibles too.

In the process, she wants to embolden Christians to speak out about their faith. She invites fans to meet her on the field after a performance. She encourages the fans, telling them, "It's not just me sharing the talents God has given me; it's wherever God has placed each one of you." She emphasizes that each person has a God-given talent and a very special place in this world.

Her second goal is similar. "When you have that ministry as your goal it makes you play the ball game in a different way. We play hard and we want to win. I am serious and my opponents are serious, too. If they could knock me out of the box, they would."

Male spectators lick their chops, expecting to get a hit off Rosie, but most go away hungry. Recognizing that desire, in early promotions Rosie's father Royal Beaird—who also served as Queen and Her Court promoter—offered five dollars to any randomly chosen spectator who could hit a fair ball. Few could. It's hard to get on board with Cracklin' Rosie. The fans who tried could take home a souvenir program and the memory that they had faced the Queen, but rarely could they say they got a hit. Twenty-five years later, five dollars may not seem like much, but don't forget, large soft drinks cost only a dime in 1964.

Gradually the stakes were raised: ten dollars a hit, then up to a hundred dollars in an exhibition at the Anaheim convention center across from Disneyland. And it wasn't a Mickey Mouse offer. None could hit. Finally a Japanese newspaper put up ten thousand dollars to entice a team of Japanese baseball professionals to face her.

Rosie claims it took five years of negotiations to get the Japanese major leaguers scheduled. The games were played in the Tokyo Giants Stadium and the Lotte Orions Stadium. "All that stuff about the male honor really was true—they didn't want to get beat." According to press accounts, a Japanese prime-time national TV audience of thirty million watched. It's not hard to guess who won.

> When I went back to second base for the stunt where I pitch from second base to make it easier [and they still can't hit it!], the manager of the team came running out protesting because he thought I was trying to embarrass his team—so I had to move back to the mound.
> They were excellent defensively and there were some good hitters, but baseball players aren't the hardest ones to strike out. They don't see risers and they don't see all the junk and, for that matter, they don't see balls being thrown from between your legs.

While in the Orient, Rosie also beat the Japanese women's national fast-pitch team 8–1, with the only run being scored when Rosie pitched from second base. "The AAA fast-pitch players and the guys who go to the World Tournament are the toughest because they have someone throwing at 90 or 100 miles per hour, too."

Nevertheless, you ask how would Rosie fare against the best male softball players? In a 1976 Memorial Day tournament Rosie took the mound with the men's Lakewood City (California) Jets, runners-up in the ISC World Tournament against an International Softball Congress All-Star team, and shut them out, winning 6–0. Case closed.

She's been married since 1986 to 6-foot-7-inch Orange County businessman Dan Schoepf, a former junior college basketball player. He was an answer to her prayers to "finally marry someone who loves God and adores me." Rosie's life appears blissful: In the summertime she travels, enjoying her unique career. In the off season she works in her husband's sign business, bakes cookies, does needlework, or curls up with a good book. She spends winters in mild-weathered Southern California, where she attends church and fellowships with Christian friends.

A 5-foot-9-inch blue-eyed blonde, Rosie is fun-loving and spirited, radiant and cheerful. In every pregame show, she announces why she is so radiant.

"Happiness is not just worldly success or winning a ball game or the prestige and glamour that goes along with being in the entertainment business. You can have all that and still not be happy. The only way I have found lasting peace and contentment is through my Lord and Savior Jesus Christ." She quotes John 3:16, and then with a wave of her hand, she's off, grabbing her glove and jogging to the mound, ready to battle that night's apprehensive roster.

The effervescence belies the struggles that have taken place in her life.

Life wasn't always so rosy.

In conversations she'll tell you candidly that her life has been one of overcoming deep hurts. "It's certainly not a perfect life, but it's one of overcoming through Jesus Christ and keeping your focus. If you get off the track, you need to get right back up and keep going on with Jesus. I hope that is the encouragement I can give to people."

Over her twenty-five-year career, most of Rosie's fans have been unaware of her father's angry abuse and of how she coped with two broken marriages and persevered through the pain of her father's death.

Rosie, the oldest daughter in a family of five—including sisters Eileen and Karen and brothers Marv and Norm—was born in Southern California. Royal and Jerry Beaird, her parents, lived in a poor Los Angeles neighborhood synonymous today with slums: Watts. Her father would play in fast-pitch softball leagues three or four nights a week, pitching or playing the field. It was his chance to be a star. Born last of twelve children, Royal grew up in an underprivileged family that shuttled between Utah and Texas. But his family was just as poor in one state as they were in the other. Nothing seemed to work for them.

Rosie, Marv, and Eileen, his oldest kids, would entertain themselves at Royal's games by playing in the dirt and running up and down the bleachers. But Rosie, ten by then, observed enough that when she signed up for a Los Angeles recreation league in 1963, she was immediately made the pitcher. She had wanted to be the shortstop.

The coaches lined everybody up at the tryouts and while the other girls gently aimed and dropped it in, Rosie says she fired back and let it rip. "All I had ever seen was a windmill style of pitching and the first thing I did was go all the way around. I just thought that was the way pitchers pitched." With some further training from her pleased father, Rosie went undefeated as her team won its league.

Rose had speed first and gained accuracy later, reminiscent of incomparable major league pitcher Nolan Ryan. Once while

Rosie was on the mound, a little girl began sobbing as she approached the plate. "I hadn't even pitched a ball and she broke down crying," Rosie recalls. The coaches came running onto the field, fearing the worst. "Did she throw it, did she hit you, what happened?"

"No she didn't throw it, but I'm just afraid," the little girl cried.

Striking out batters and winning was fun. But when Rosie tried to sign up the following season, league officials asked her to please not play because she was too good. "None of the other girls would play if I signed up so they barred me from the league," says Rosie.

No matter.

Royal Beaird just sponsored his own tournaments through the Rolling Hills Kids Klub, enticing teams with prize monies of up to a hundred dollars to take on his youngsters. The Kids Klub branched out into other youth activities besides sports: talent and photography contests and mountain trips. Along with the physical training, Royal Beaird taught spiritual and moral values and encouraged the kids to have high standards and principles.

While those activities were fun, softball was number one. Following a 1964 City Championship game, one spectator was overheard saying, "Boy, with that pitcher and catcher, who needs a team—they could win all alone!" Thus was born the Queen and Her Court. Besides Rosie and her sister Eileen, two other players were added, but more for offensive purposes. "If you get the bases loaded you need one more person at the plate," Rosie offers, smiling. A first baseman covers the entire right side of the diamond and a shortstop covers the left. Other modifications include outfield cones placed 225 feet from home plate that designate home runs and ground-rule doubles, an hour-and-a-half time limit, and a designated hitter for Rosie. But it's not like she's an actress with an understudy. Without Rosie, and Rosie alone, the show couldn't go on.

By 1965 Rosie and Eileen had traveled eighteen thousand miles as members of the Queen and Her Court. The original itinerary included only Utah and Texas, but requests for the unique quartet kept pouring in and they eventually criss-crossed the United States and Canada. As the troupe sharpened its act, a crazy comedy clown character, Lotta Chatter, was added for entertainment and to keep the scores closer and more exciting. How perfect: touring worldwide, competing, appearing on television shows from "Truth or Consequences" to the "Tonight Show with Johnny Carson" to Merv Griffin and Mike Douglas. How many teenagers get to do that? But this perfect lifestyle carried a high price, according to Rosie.

> From the time the bell rang after school, we were on the field practicing. My dad was strict about practicing. When we had that Kids Klub we had lots of friends. But when we got to high school we didn't have that circle anymore. I was kind of introverted yet because I could do something well, my dad pushed me to perform and be up front. If it hadn't been for the softball thing, I think I would have been very introverted. I pleaded and I was nervous and scared and tense.

But why, she is asked.

> We feared not doing well. There was a great deal of tension and I thought when I was young, "If only I can get out of this."
>
> Those instances of dealing with my dad's anger left me with a lot of scars and hurts and it shaped my life. Between me and God, I accept responsibility for all the rebellion and all the bad decisions I made, but I can look back and know why I made them. At the time being rebellious was the best choice I could come up with.
>
> Most kids have parents that don't spend any time with them. My dad spent every waking moment with us. Of course I didn't want all that. He was always affectionate; he just disciplined harshly.

Her parents divorced when she was sixteen, and the three older children, Rosie, Marv, and Eileen, lived with their father during the week, and then joined Karen and Norm at their mother's on the weekends. Rosie felt like it was two days to relax away from her ever-present and critical father.

In addition to the daily practice ritual which consumed any time for friendships, Rosie was not allowed to date until she was nearly eighteen. She wasn't allowed to attend the prom—because it came during softball season. And her father accompanied her to high school football games, further decreasing her chances to socialize.

"People would come up to me and say, 'You're the luckiest person in the world. I wish I could do what you're doing.' And I was. I was. But in my mind I would say, 'I wish you really knew. You wouldn't want to do this for anything.'" Parts were exciting—traveling, being in the entertainment field, competing and striving for accomplishment. "When you strike somebody out, you are just going, 'Yeah, this is fun. It feels great!'" Emotions like that can disappear quickly, however, overwhelmed by hurt feelings and painful memories.

For example, what should have been a thrilling experience playing in a major league stadium was soured by too much negative pressure from her father. Rosie received a special invitation to showcase her talents in the then-new Houston Astrodome. Yes, it would be exciting to be thirteen years old and pitching before a crowd of thirty thousand.

Rosie recalls that experience with mixed feelings. "I about wet my pants before I got onto the field. I had to go to the bathroom so many times. It was thrilling, but at the same time people were saying, 'Aren't you scared to be in front of all those people? You're so young, aren't you afraid of them?' Heck no, I was afraid of my dad over there with the microphone! That was my motivation."

Fear of her father influenced Rosie in other ways. She first married at age twenty to get out of the house.

> I had a heart for God and I loved God, but I didn't have a lot of wisdom. I just made a really dumb decision. I guess I had never dated much. And he said he was a Christian. I wanted a Christian and I wanted someone fun. I didn't want a stereotype of what everyone thinks—that Christians are no fun. I just wanted to get out of my dad's control. I had no life of my own. Everything was what he wanted and I felt that was my only way out.
>
> My first husband was very insecure and his dad even said to me that he just didn't have a good self-image, that if he was the governor of California he would still feel inadequate. I was trying my hardest to make him happy.

With that divorce came more problems, both spiritually and with her father. "I thought I'd never be able to serve God again. It's like some sins are in red neon lights, flashing: divorce, divorce, divorce. I felt like I was a leper. I have never had drugs, never smoked or tried it, and I have never even tasted alcohol because of the way we were brought up." Royal ruled out of love and a desire to protect his children but then he became erratic and irrational and his temper increased.

Offers to do lucrative beer commercials on TV today don't tempt her because of her committed faith.

"I said no because that's the connotation everybody gets about softball: bring out the keg and whoever wins gets the keg. Not all the money in the world is worth it to me because that would be what the public would remember Rosie Black for—not as the one who is a good athlete and plays softball to serve Jesus Christ and for the glory of God. They'd only remember, 'Didn't she do that beer commercial?'"

The consummate professional, like the clown who hides his tears, Rosie persevered throughout her personal troubles, maintaining her arduous pitching schedule. "During parts of my life where I thought I was going to have a nervous breakdown, I still performed and no one knew except the people close to me. In that, I was a total professional."

But Rosie was still searching for love in all the wrong places, trying to fill that void created by her father's criticism. Not long afterwards she got married again, perhaps too quickly, she admits now, realizing she hadn't fully healed from the emotional trauma of the first broken marriage. However, once again Royal's interference proved disruptive.

> Probably if my dad had not been there, we would still be married. But here I was, thirty years old and I didn't want to be without a husband to protect me or my dad might swing on me. We all had to travel together, and my dad was constantly critical. I could pretend to get along but my exhusband couldn't. I'd always done it. But he couldn't do it. He got so nervous that he would almost break out in hives.

It took Rosie a few more years and her father's passing away to genuinely understand that pretending of that sort was unhealthy.

"That young man was one of the best athletes I've seen and I admired him so much. He was incredible. We played some of the hardest teams during that time and he would go 9 for 10. Despite his hitting so well, my dad would review the books the next day and criticize him. But he was the one that helped us win all those games. He'd come up every four batters and he was so fast you couldn't stop him on the bases," she recalls.

The young man played with the Queen and Her Court for four years and they were married for two and a half years, but he finally told Rosie that he couldn't handle her father anymore; that it was their marriage or softball. Rosie feared not pleasing her father more than the loss of a husband. When so-called parental love is abusive, children—no matter the age—will still equate it with real love since that's all they've known. And Rosie couldn't break that shackle.

Moreover, Rosie knew her father's wishes that she not have children; fearing him, she complied. No play, no pay. Guilt and fear added unbearable pressure. "My ex-spouse asked me to quit the team and make some other changes, and I told him the other things I could do but I couldn't quit the team." For Rosie, that would be like quitting her family, which depended on her to play the starring role. As Rosie has matured, she's gained insight into those problems.

"My dream wasn't God's dream. I had an idea of what would work. I wanted my career to work, and to keep playing I would have to have my husband go with me to be my protector. I didn't want to be alone playing softball."

After her second marriage dissolved, Rosie again tried to work things out with her father. "He always wanted to be so close, close, close but when I got married he thought I wasn't being close. It was as though I was alienating him and my marriage had caused the division between father and daughter. I was really doing my best to make my husband happy and my dad happy, and it seemed like I was always caught in the middle."

Royal had failed to accept Genesis 2:24, about newlyweds leaving their parents and cleaving to their spouses.

"He told me he thought it was neat that we could finally be close again and communicate and talk. I really hadn't communicated any differently, but because I could be there twenty-four hours a day he thought I had changed." Change was only in the eyes of the beholder.

Sometimes in return, Rosie needed her father's genuine help and interest. For instance, every preseason she anxiously doubted whether she "still had it" or whether she'd forgotten every pitch over the winter. Like climbing on a bicycle again, she'd always rediscover her talent. But that particular spring Rosie suffered shooting pains from knee to toe which hampered her throwing and she genuinely hurt. "All I wanted was the sympathy that a friend will give and supposedly he was saying that now that we are friends we can do this."

Royal brusquely dismissed her concern, and told her to keep on pitching. Because of that rebuff and others Rosie resolved never to share anything consequential with him again. "I'm not going to say one honest truthful thing about my feelings," she remembers thinking. "I was really hurt. He said he wanted to know my feelings, from friend to friend, but he'd never listen." Later a shoe problem was discovered and corrected and the physical pains ceased, but inside, Rosie still hurt.

But there was One who would listen—her Lord Jesus Christ—

and she turned to Him. "I prayed, and prayed, and prayed. I talked to the Lord. During those hard times, He got to be my best friend. All I did day and night for at least a couple of months was read my Bible. I didn't do anything else. I was probably close to a nervous breakdown. I didn't go by myself anywhere."

Despite her success on the diamond, for the second time Rosie found herself alone and feeling like a failure. Her sister Eileen, three years younger, also provided a welcome listening ear. And her mother, Jerry, provided unconditional love and reminded Rosie about Jesus' unconditional love.

Rosie tells how she wanted to get on that right path that God plans, but because of circumstances and choices, she'd always get off it. "You can always get back on that plan He has for you, but coming back is a hard old road. So I said to the Lord, 'Please Lord, stop me this time. Knock me in the head. I don't want to get off on a sidetrack anymore.'"

Physical problems affected her, too. She couldn't sleep, so she tried sleeping pills. But she was still too nervous. When the first dose didn't seem to help she took some more and finally crashed. But at 2:00 the next afternoon she awoke unrefreshed and recalls thinking, "I don't know how God wants me to recover emotionally and get back on track, but sleeping pills aren't the answer. So if I have to stay up all night I'm going to be praying and reading. I don't like the way I feel right now. I'm so drugged out. This isn't what God wants me to do. If He can't help me get some sleep at night, I'll stay up with Him." Over the course of the next few months, reading her Bible, praying, and seeking biblically based professional counseling helped her recover.

Eileen, a committed believer, also gave Rosie some sound advice about potential suitors. "Look into the man's life and see how he loves the Lord and how he treats you. If you'll just wait and give it time you will see how that person is."

While Rosie grew in the depth of her relationship with the Lord, she recognized a bad habit that interfered with genuine communication. "I had to learn to overcome clicking off my mind when I was getting yelled and screamed at. That was the way I coped with problems with my dad and my husbands. To cope I would go into a kind of comatose state with my brain, which is a really horrible, devastating habit. If you want to be a full, vibrant person for the Lord, you just can't do that."

During that period of her life she began to understand the power of the Holy Spirit. With that excitement and freedom in her relationship with the Lord, she wondered about the purpose of softball. She wanted to serve God wholeheartedly. Should she continue to play?

> Eileen helped me see that this was how I was serving Him. When I first started pitching, I'd share Christ with every reporter in interviews, but later I found out that it almost always got cut out of the article. I was discouraged because it seemed like hardly anyone knew what I stood for. That's when Eileen encouraged me to say something over the microphone, so I began to think and pray about that.

Not long afterwards she woke up about 3:00 A.M. with an idea of what she should say. "I wrote it down on a piece of paper because I knew I'd forget it by morning. It was almost verbatim what I say now and have been saying before games.

"Every once in a while we ran the risk of losing a booking, but to this day it's more important to us to be able to share our faith."

She has strong feelings about that. "Others share Buddha, and Mohammad, and things like spiritual channelings, so why can't I share what I believe?" Audiences are attentive as Rosie sincerely shares her personal message.

Following the 1984 tour, Royal suffered a heart attack, along with a severe depression. He forever wanted to be young and vibrant and involved in playing sports.

"He couldn't handle the illness and getting older very well. And I think he felt a little guilty about a lot of stuff that happened in his life. Unresolved guilt can severely depress you. To him everything looked like it was going downhill when actually it wasn't." He told Rosie he hesitated about traveling because of his heart problem, and he complained of tremendous headaches, nerves, and pain. "He'd only perk up when, for instance, buddies at the gym would come and talk to him. A lot of the pain was caused by burying guilt and emotional things. He was just negative all the time."

Rosie was concerned enough about his health to stay with him for several weeks, and then weekends only as he gradually improved. While taking care of him, she hoped to clear up her ugly feelings about the abuse she'd received, but Royal couldn't understand the extent of her feelings.

The abuse had caused Rosie to become an overachiever. She never felt her best was good enough. Although she racked up incredible achievements in her career, she never truly thought she was measuring up. "People think, 'Oh, the great Rosie Black,' but part of me thought I wasn't good at all," she recalls.

While in some ways Royal was a genius as a coach, she says, he also was difficult to understand. "He did some things so perfect. That's probably why I'm as good as I am. If I'd say I couldn't strike a person out, he'd tell me there was always a way to get a person. Sure enough, he would give me a tip and I would do it and it would work." Rosie calls him an excellent trainer who taught her every pitch she throws. "He couldn't throw it, but he could explain it to me; he was a good teacher." He was patient to work with young pitchers who begged him to teach them a pitch following her summertime exhibitions. But there was no patience with his own children.

While Royal refined Rosie's pitching skills, he was cunningly calculating. Royal astutely selected teams that would challenge her prowess but not beat her, so that she would always win, building her confidence. Early in her career he pitted her against teenage boys in a local park, then as she improved, against men's nine-player teams, and finally against professional baseball stars such as Johnny Bench and Willie Mays. All had the same result: lots of air as they swung, then turning to see the ball in the catcher's mitt.

"We would go to the park when I was thirteen or fourteen and he would round up all the guys and we would strike out lines of them." For the boys it was better than going to the batting cages. No cost, except perhaps a bruised ego.

In February 1985, Rosie's father passed away, but the Queen and Her Court had obligations to play games. That summer, however, they had an unusual break in their schedule. And it was cheaper to fly home to Southern California than to stay on the road.

"That *never* happened," says Rosie. "Usually we were gone for three straight months."

When they arrived, a friend invited her to a party. While others were drinking, Rosie noticed that an athletic-looking man named Dan and his friend weren't. She and Dan started talking and he mentioned something about prayer. The two discovered they were both Christians; yet, Rosie was cautious, influenced by Eileen's wise words.

As they chatted, Rosie discovered Dan had been raised in a Christian home, but had gotten sidetracked into alcohol and drug abuse. With the help of Alcoholics Anonymous, Dan had quit using alcohol and other drugs. Rosie could support Dan in his efforts to maintain a sober lifestyle, and Dan could encourage Rosie to deal with her past troubles with her father. "The main thing," Rosie says, "is this really super-sweet, nice, friendly new guy treated me like a lady. But I thought if we got married it would be different." Doubts lingered from her previous marital failures, but through Dan's steadfast love, his consistency, his trust in the Lord, God removed those obstacles and in time Dan and Rosie got married.

> Dan is a total sweetheart, but when he and I first got married, I would "click him off" when we disagreed because it was a habit. Then I repented and said I was sorry, and explained what I was doing so he could help me. I said, "When you raised your voice at me, my heart started to pound a little bit and I went 'click,' and tuned out. I just didn't hear a word you said and therefore I can't communicate with you right now. I don't know what's happening. I've been yelled at so long that I can't even talk when there's any kind of disagreement."

Dan's gentle understanding has helped Rosie overcome that earlier conditioning, and his faithful support has helped her blossom beyond the playing field. They are considering having children or possibly adopting, and Rosie recognizes that Dan would be a good father. But as long as she's able and with Dan's blessing, while he operates his sign business in Southern California, she'll still be "the Queen," entertaining fans and sharing her genuine love for the Lord.

Rosie concludes,

> As I've matured in Christ I've discovered that I may never understand the answers to hard questions in my life. Instead, I choose to look daily to a loving God who is completely worthy of my undivided trust in Him, no matter what.
>
> He promises to work all that has happened to me for my good if I'll love Him and try to fit into His plans. Not one shred of my life was a waste, and what could have been evil and destructive, God used for His glory.

Olympic Gold Medalist, Swimmer
Anna Johnson (photo by Tim
Davis Photography)

Professional Triathlete and Two-Time National
Champion Kirsten Hanssen Ames

Olympic and NCAA Champion
Gretchen Magers (photo by Carol
L. Newsom)

Olympic Ice Skater Caryn Kadavy

ABOVE: All-American and Olympic
Volleyball Player Debbie Brown
LEFT: Gold-Medal-Winning, Women's
Olympic Basketball Coach Kay Yow

Four-Time Olympic
speedskater Nancy
Swider-Peltz (far right)
with President Reagan
(holding her daughter
Nancy), and Olympic
teammates Dan Jansen
and Bonnie Blair

# 9 *Caryn Kadavy*

## The winner's edge

SOME MAY SAY THAT Caryn Kadavy (pronounced kuh-*day*-vee), international ice-skating star turned professional, is living on the edge. Oh, she may not be driving race cars at 220 miles per hour or riding steers at the rodeo. After all, she's living on a different kind of edge—a thin edge of cold steel only ⅛ of an inch thick.

Skating titles may be won or lost over tiny ruts (which may seem to resemble the Grand Canyon to the athlete who has tripped over them) left by previous skaters. It's all a matter of timing—and a bit of luck. And all the while it's smile, smile, smile.

Caryn's skating career teeters on that thin edge that separates winners from losers. Her competition is a one-shot pressurized chance to impress judges by combining choreographed balletic flair with acrobatic athleticism. With keen-eyed judges and worldwide audiences numbering in the tens of millions for some events, skaters are truly thrust onto a thin edge of confidence.

For skaters, there are no overtimes to regain momentum as there are in basketball. There are no extra innings, penalty kicks, or stopwatches to determine the winner's edge.

When the spotlight is on, it's time to shine. And if you're feeling a little down that day, ahem, cough, cough, maaaaaybe there's next year.

Caryn, now twenty-two, has seen both sides in her five-year international amateur career. After bagging four international titles after reaching the Senior Ladies level at age sixteen—including the Skate Canada and the Moscow (USSR) Prize News tournaments in 1985, the Golden Spin of Zagreb (Yugoslavia) in

1986, and the 1987 St. Ivel (England) International—and after representing the United States at three World Championships and the Goodwill Games and winning a spot on the 1988 Winter Olympic Team, she felt positioned to break into the elite grouping of East Germany's Katarina Witt, America's Debi Thomas, and Canada's Elizabeth Manley.

A third-place finish and bronze medal in the 1987 World Championships in Cincinnati buoyed those hopes. Instead, her fairy-tale scenario of bursting onto the international ice skating scene blurred. If there had been a televised game show featuring as hostess the lovely and gracious 5-foot-5-inch, petite, green-eyed brunette, the pride of Erie, Pennsylvania, the new show could have been aptly titled "Name that Malady."

When it was her day in the sun to shine, the weather was partly cloudy. But in the process of dealing with adversity, Caryn has learned to trust God even more and allow Him to guide her life.

At the 1988 Olympics in Calgary, Caryn was excited, and hopeful of winning a medal. She had worked hard to improve her program between the nationals and the Olympics and felt everything was prepared. Marching in with the team during the opening ceremonies was uplifting. Even living in the Olympic Village (despite eight girls sharing a bathroom) was fun, she says.

But along with meeting new friends, she met up with an unwelcome virus. With figure skating's glamorous men's and women's singles being the last event, there was just enough time for the Asian flu strains and the European flu viruses to make the rounds and have a convention in Caryn's G.I. tract. Neither medication nor rest could dispel the 103.5-degree fever, vomiting, chills, and severe headache.

Although weakened, Caryn skated the preliminary school figures and completed the short program with a 101-degree temperature which subsequently went up. "I rested as well as I could and felt pretty good after that. I felt I had the energy so I went out and did a good short program," she comments. "I'm thankful that I have those memories of just being able to skate at the Olympics." She recuperated with her family, including her parents Don and Marlene, and sister Carla, at their Calgary host family's home, hopeful that it might be only a twenty-four-hour flu.

But the illness persisted and Caryn was forced to withdraw prior to the finals. ABC-TV interviewed her from her sickroom and she glumly shared her disappointment with a nationwide audience.

Looking back, Caryn recalls the dashed hopes, but says that through that experience she learned a lot about being content.

Through things like losing, you ask God, "Why?" and wonder, "Is God out there working for me?" I've been through the doubting stages where you doubt yourself as well as God, but the main thing I've learned is to go out and skate to the best of the ability God has given me.

We are always so hard on ourselves to try to be more than we are. We always want to strive for more, sure, and to be our best. But we can also be greedy in wrong ways—in putting success, not character, first. I've learned that through my years of skating. I'm still learning and growing in that every day.

I want to try to look at my life as much as possible from the eyes of God. It's hard, because we all get distracted in a lot of ways, but I try to believe in Him and in His Word. I also want Him to be pleased with who I am before the Lord.

I know He's looking over me in my skating and in my life, too. God knew what He was doing when He gave me my first break. My dream became to make the Olympics—and I did it!

And she lightly adds, "But I forgot to tell Him I would like a medal!"

Caryn began skating on double runners around the time most toddlers learn to walk. Her parents, Don, a research chemist, and Marlene, a former ballerina, and older sister Carla, would ice skate for recreation by their home on Presque Isle Peninsula near Lake Erie. Soon they joined the Westminster Skating Club of Erie, where they would push little Caryn around the rink. At age four, she began tagging along for their weekly lessons and loved it. But the indoor rink had ice for only the six winter months of the year, so in the off season Caryn busied herself with swimming and ballet. However it was skating she truly enjoyed, even the time-consuming school figures so detestable to many skaters. Caryn loved their preciseness and being able to measure her gains.

She says, "I did enjoy it because I got such a sense of accomplishment out of it. If I didn't have a great day, I'd pick out the best thing that I did, even if it was figures, because that was an important part of skating, too.

"Carla skated a little bit before I took it up and passed a few tests, but she really didn't like it. She didn't like to jump or do the compulsory figures," says Caryn, proudly noting her sister's accomplishments as a gifted pianist, talented artist, and athlete. "She loved all sports. She didn't just pick one like me.

"But I loved everything about skating. I mean, that's all I would dream about—skating, skating, skating." Her parents regularly drove her two hours to Pittsburgh for additional lessons and test sessions, and sometimes she would stay with her grandparents and attend summer sessions in order to pass more USFSA (United States Figure Skating Association) tests. Each advancement meant new stickers for her USFSA book and patches for her jackets and bulletin board. At age seven she passed her first big step by completing three serpentine circles within a figure-eight design.

By the time she was ten years old, she started year-round training and explains, "For instance, in Rockford [Illinois, where she's lived and trained], they have summer ice school and kids can come here or go to similar ice rinks for additional training and academics if they don't want to stay home during the school year." While in Pittsburgh she met instructor Charlene Minneci Guarino, who encouraged Don and Marlene to further develop Caryn's talents on the ice, particularly her jumps. One day's lessons convinced them to seek further training with Charlene.

"Maybe she didn't think there was any hope for me that I'd improve so quickly, but she couldn't believe how fast I picked up on it," Caryn recalls. "And I couldn't believe how glad I was to be able to do a jump so easily!" Caryn also trained in Colorado Springs at the Broadmoor World Arena.

In skating there's no age group competition—just pass your tests and you're in. Skaters progress from basic to intermediate, novice, junior, and senior levels. Each of three sectional championships (Eastern, Midwest, and Pacific Coast) that determine participants in the nationals are made up of three regionals. The New England, North Atlantic, and South Atlantic Regionals send their qualifiers to the Eastern Championships. The Eastern Great Lakes, Upper Great Lakes, and Southwestern send their qualifiers to the Midwestern Championships. And the winners of the Northwest, Central, and Southwest Pacific Regionals go to the Pacific Coast Championships.

Regionals are generally in November, sectionals in January, and nationals—every skater's dream—in February, with the World Championships in March. The top four skaters in each regional qualify for the sectionals, with the top four in each section qualifying for nationals. Each skater is required to perform selected compulsory figures, commonly called school figures (these will be done away with in Olympic and world competition after 1990), a short free-skating program featuring certain required moves, and the flashy long program.

At age twelve, Caryn competed in the North Atlantic Regionals, but didn't make the final round. Judges, coaches, and spectators saw her potential and encouraged her to stay with it. "They always told us she had national potential," says Marlene. "She had a certain style when she was very, very young."

For the next two years Caryn shuttled between the Broadmoor and Rockford, former home of Olympian and seven-time national champion Janet Lynn. Living with host families like a foreign exchange student proved unworkable, so Marlene accompanied her and set up house while Caryn trained.

Finally, at age fourteen, Caryn qualified in juniors for the Midwestern Sectionals by placing third in the Upper Great Lakes Regional. An unexpected and disappointing fifth-place finish there caused her to reconsider the hardships she was placing on her family.

"We were giving up hope and thinking about quitting because it was too much money," says Caryn, who wondered when she was ever going to make it to the top. At that time skates were "only" five hundred dollars a pair (and you needed two pairs) and had to be replaced every six months because "you were constantly on them and the leather wore out" and lessons were "only" thirty-five dollars an hour. (Entering the 1990s, those expenses are easily double and triple that amount.) But while competing in the Midwestern Sectionals, Caryn attracted the eye of Carlo Fassi, talent hunter extraordinaire and former coach of famed world and Olympic champions Peggy Fleming, Dorothy Hamill, John Curry, and Robin Cousins.

"He thought I was one of the best skaters there and wanted to take me on as a student," she says. "I was ecstatic!" On his next trip through Chicago, while traveling to the World Championships, Carlo met Caryn and Marlene at O'Hare International Airport and arranged to take her on. That summer she passed her eighth and final test to qualify for the Senior Ladies and pursued even more intense training with Fassi.

By 1985, at age seventeen, she had added more triple jumps to her program, qualified for nationals by winning the Southwesterns, and on her first trip to the nationals in Kansas City, confidently displayed her improvement. She finished third, and became an alternate for the World Championships (only two qualify, plus a third if one person is the defending world medalist). It was unusual

for a skater to place nationally without having been "seen" previously or having developed a name by continually winning sectional
or regional titles. The exposure of working out with Carlo Fassi at
the mecca of ice skating, the Broadmoor, had paid off.

Still, expenses were escalating. Marlene, with Don's support,
stayed in Chicago and worked in real estate, sending stipends
to Colorado Springs for Caryn and Carla. The United States
Olympic Committee generates some support for potential skaters,
but at the time the skaters had to be titlists to qualify. In addition
there are sponsors who help by providing trust funds from which
to pay expenses. One such donor was a woman whom Caryn had
met during an open skating session, who was able to support her
anonymously. "She didn't want me to know for the longest time
because she didn't want me to feel obligated to her," says Caryn.
"We just skated together and became good friends and I just never
knew it was her that was helping me out."

Living with Carla in Colorado Springs was fun, Caryn recalls.
"When Carla and I were talking recently, we were laughing and
saying that was the best summer of our lives." Carla, then a
nineteen-year old college student, played housemom. "For the
longest time, it was really the only summer we spent together
because I was always away for summer school."

Her bronze medal at Nationals may not have been Caryn's
ticket to the World Championships, but it did earn her a trip to
Canada for an international competition in which she defeated
1988 Olympic-silver-medalist-to-be Elizabeth Manley, and another trip to the Soviet Union, where she again won. It was the
first time in ten years the Americans had sent a delegation to the
Moscow Prize News competition. "My coach said if we win that's
fabulous because nobody's ever done it before," says Caryn.
"Those were good international experiences for me since I had
never been to a world competition. It kind of set up the next year
for me."

In 1986 Caryn improved to second nationally, behind Debi
Thomas, and qualified for her initial World Championship,
where she finished a disappointing eighth because of a heel injury.
Because there was not sufficient time to buy and break in new
skates, Caryn had an old pair rebuilt. Unfortunately, too much
added padding in the heel put faulty pressure on the arch and
injured her heel. Later that summer she represented the United
States again, along with Thomas, Tiffany Chin, Brian Boitano,
Scott Gregory, and Christopher Bowman, at the Goodwill Games

in Moscow which was an ice skating exhibition rather than a competition.

During that time period Caryn had cosmetic surgery on her nose to correct some lumps and accentuate her appearance. "I was always self-conscious in pictures and interviews," she says. "I had the surgery done to correct some previous injuries to my nose. A skater's looks are important, but I did it mainly for me—it just wasn't attractive." Just part of the game plan, coach. Such cosmetic improvements are known and accepted in skating.

All things seemed to be pointing upwards for Caryn. Yet back in Colorado Springs another skater, Jill Trenary, attracted attention by winning the junior nationals. For Caryn it was hard sharing her coach with the highly-acclaimed newcomer. "Carlo couldn't say to me, 'I want you to beat the pants off Jill Trenary,' because she was his skater, too," Caryn recalls.

Jill followed up on her 1986 junior title by winning the 1987 Senior Ladies, beating defending champion Thomas. Caryn, skating last that evening, came through with a stunning long program with a Spanish theme to cement third place and another trip to the World Championships. Three Americans would enter because of Thomas's medal the previous year.

*Skating Magazine* wrote that Caryn "knew what had to be done and reached deep within to maintain the concentration of a championship competitor. With her customary elegant body lines and attention to details, marks of 5.4 to 5.9 for a beautifully choreographed program that included a difficult triple loop-double toe, triple toe and Salchow pulled her up one place over Chin for the bronze."[1]

Caryn had qualified for the World Championships and could quietly train on with the simple attitude of trying to be the best she could be. Jill would have to face the added pressure of meeting public and press requests.

"I trained my heart out before the '87 World Championships. I told myself I didn't care where I placed, just that I wanted to skate the best I could. I knew that I could skate, and in particular, do better figures and a better short program than I did at nationals." Caryn fulfilled her goal and finished a triumphant third, behind Witt and Thomas, while Jill slipped to seventh. Afterwards, Caryn got added skating exposure from an invitation

---

1. *Skating Magazine*, vol. 64, no. 4 (April 1987):36.

to join the World Tour, appearing with ice skating's elite in exhibitions in over thirty cities.

Caryn muses, "Perhaps I did better internationally than nationally because I was more of a European-looking skater. I think the Europeans admired my skating style, which helped me do well there. I went through a time when I was confused and wondered whether I should try to imitate Debi and Jill and their athleticism or try to be myself. You can't look like someone else, but skating was evolving into more athleticism and it was hard for me to know how to proceed competitively."

Marlene adds her thoughts. "Caryn has a very soft feminine look about her and even though she faced criticism for not being tough and aggressive, she was tough internally," she says. "We couldn't change her long line if we'd wanted to."

With her magnificent performance at the 1987 World Championships, Caryn showed that you don't have to look like a barracuda on the outside to be as tough as a barracuda on the inside. Tied for fourth going into the free skating with Canada's impressive Liz Manley, she dug deep for another stunning finale to win the bronze medal.

The next year she spent preparing for the Calgary Olympics, only to face that keen disappointment when she had to drop out because of the flu. An added sinus infection and an allergic reaction to the medication compounded her miseries and she felt unprepared for the World Championships in March in Budapest.

At Fassi's urging she entered anyway, but finished seventh. By the year's end, despite a relaxing summer hiatus and an enjoyable vacation, she'd had a tonsillectomy to cure residual problems from her previous winter's illnesses and also surgery to remove an ovarian cyst.

Many would have succumbed to discouragement, but instead Caryn sees that rough and unfortunate year as a character builder.

I'd never experienced so many illnesses or so many injuries. All those things just happened. As athletes, we're not almighty and we're not robots either. We're people first before we get into skating, and we just have to accept those kinds of things.

It took me back a little bit and made me realize that I should be thankful for what shape I was in, for what point I could get to and that I was able to do so many triples in my program—one of my main goals.

I remember wishing then I could do more or work harder. It's hard to explain, but as each day goes by I think I'm beginning to just accept what's happened.

Through the trials and disappointments, Caryn has maintained the sweet disposition that makes her popular with fellow skaters through a steadfastness that reveals her personal relationship with Jesus Christ. A poster on her wall proclaiming, "With God all things are possible," reflects her trust in a higher source.

"At one point in my career I was so on top and physically and mentally confident. Then going through the trauma of losing my health, physical conditioning, and confidence because I wasn't up to par—that was hard. I had a lot of up and down feelings through all that.

"It's easy to take for granted how great you feel and you forget how much you should appreciate being well. If you don't have your health you can't skate. So it affects how you view yourself." Self-identity can easily be wrapped up in what you do rather than whose you are. Caryn chose to trust God through her difficulties.

"Skating is really a secondary thing. It's part of my life but I'm a person, too, and not just a skater. We all have to come to reality through these kinds of learning experiences and we have to learn to accept what God has for us. Sure, we could all sit here in a depression.

"But I look at it in a positive sense: that God will show me His way and that He'll guide me through any storm. I know I'm going to make it and that I'll wake up the next morning and life will go on. It's my choice to be happy and I can always be happy to be living. I still have all my abilities and I can grow from here, wherever I am. That's the main thing: we can all grow and strive onward."

Truly, she's a champion without a national, world, or Olympic title. In some sports an athlete might be honored with an all-conference or all-American moniker. But not so in skating. You are *the* world champion, *the* national champion, *the* Olympic champion. When it's time to negotiate professional contracts with various ice shows, only gold medals translate into marquee value.

Until November of 1989 there was only one thing that was more up in the air than Caryn's double toe loops and triple axels: the future direction of her career. Should she turn professional and begin recouping some of the outrageous expenses of an eight-year amateur career? Things like thousand dollar pairs of skates and coaching fees of up to sixty dollars an hour, plus costly custom-made costumes, patch (practice) time, and plane tickets? Or should she wait and try again to capture that elusive national title?

Finally, regaining her strength allowed Caryn to realize she wanted to turn pro. She realizes she's not a titlist but is confident that she can establish her graceful artistry as a professional.

I'm not really thinking about the amount of money to be had. I want to go out and skate for people who enjoy my style of skating. I get so much joy out of performing, and I want to continue to share that with others. Obviously, I want to be able to make some money because this will be my job. Hopefully, I'll be able to get back some of the amounts I've sacrificed to train for my sport and also help some of the people who have helped me in my career.

When I was still feeling weak I couldn't decide whether I wanted to try to go on in amateur skating or turn professional. But now I'm at a point where I can make this decision properly. I realize it's a transition into the unknown and that it's going to be tough because it's different from the amateur world. But I'm excited about it, too, because I can express myself through a different aspect than amateur skating with all its rules and competition and comparison. There is more individuality regarding music selection and freedom to express whatever type of person I want to go out there and be. That's exciting because I feel more is offered in an artistic sense.

I realize I won't make as much money as people who have won the Olympics or have been national champions. That's reality and you have to face the facts.

But some people aren't content no matter how much money they make. You never know the whole story. They may not be as happy as I am even though I'm not making as much. There's so much more involved than just money. The main thing is to find that inner peace within yourself and to be content with God.

I took my shot and all those things happened. Now I want to do something else with my skating. I looked at the competition coming up and heard the talk, and I would have been playing catch-up because of the time I was off. And then I would have had to prove myself on that one day to be number one. I knew how much that would take. I've been second, I've been third in the United States and to bet on having the judges recognize me as number one would have been risking a lot because they might have their eye on some upcoming skater.

What I really needed to accept was that if I didn't do that miracle performance on that one day, could I be happy with second or third? Everybody comes to a time in their lives when they have to accept something which perhaps they don't want to.

Turning professional means joining the Professional Skaters Guild of America, skating exhibitions, and performing in shows and benefits—perhaps up to two hundred appearances a year. Two of Caryn's favorite selections to perform to are "Ave Maria" sung by Barbra Streisand, and the "Lord's Prayer" sung by gospel singer Sandy Patti. Once, before skating an exhibition at the Broadmoor, she took the microphone and dedicated her performance to those who had inspired her. "That song—'the Lord's Prayer'—just gives you chills up and down your spine," she says.

Perhaps she doesn't have a title to hang her name on, but still she's thankful for all that skating has given her.

Marlene wistfully says with a typical mother's pride that she wants what's best for Caryn.

"I certainly think she was worthy during those years to win at least one gold medal," says Marlene. "Her talent showed itself in practice and in international competition, and yet somehow I know God had a reason. Caryn always had such a marvelous reputation and was always very good to other people." And with a mother's wisdom she concludes, "I guess it doesn't really matter, because none of the medals in the world are going to get you to heaven."

Caryn herself seems secure in accepting her career's peaks and valleys. "I've come to appreciate the downfalls because they've built my character. I've accomplished a tremendous amount and I'm thankful for that, but it's during the down times that God has really taught me how to trust Him and not give up on myself or on Him. Maybe God has allowed that so I could encourage others."

Caryn's once thin edge of confidence seems to have become a mile wide.

# 10
# Gretchen Magers

## Improving her serve

WHEN YOU ARRIVE at the home of professional tennis player Gretchen Magers and her husband, Steve, it's not just a friendly "Welcome" you'll receive, but a hearty "Welcome, aboard!"

Gretchen and Steve married on December 19, 1986 after meeting at Trinity University in San Antonio, Texas. They now live on their houseboat—the *Gypsy Lady*—moored in San Diego harbor. They had gotten to know each other through a campus group called Young Life which sponsors Christian activities for local high school students. Because of her hectic tennis schedule, Gretchen participated infrequently and from a distance admired Steve, a football running back who was one of the group's leaders.

"He was the one that gave the little speeches and talked up front with the kids. I just thought he was the greatest. I always kept in the background because I couldn't come all the time and he was one of the vocal ones. I admired him for being able to get up and lead songs and talk in front of the kids—that was something I thought I couldn't do. He was funny and they really liked him and responded to him." When Steve and Gretchen took a comparative anatomy class together they became lab partners, which led to their becoming life partners.

Like many young Southern California couples they were priced out of the expensive housing market—until they happened onto the houseboat. (Most appropriately they munch on Cap'n Crunch cereal for breakfast.) It's tight but there's room for all the modern toys and necessities. After all, this is not the Mayflower.

Complete with kitchen, bedroom, dining room, bathroom, computer room, study, sundeck, and guest quarters—all condensed into about 300 square feet—their miniyacht has room for even their black labrador retriever. It's an adventure for sure, but it's "home, sweet, home." Steve and Gretchen save for the future by driving small older model cars. When their schedules permit, the Magerses enjoy sailing around San Diego's waters.

Sure, after hot and humid San Antonio, it's an adjustment in more ways than you can shake a tennis racket at, but while Gretchen travels to tournaments, Steve works on his master's degree in exercise physiology at San Diego State. Gretchen, originally from Pittsburgh, and Steve, a Houston native, say they'd like to stay on the West Coast "if they can afford it." In this case, bloom where you're planted means imitating a water lily.

Although she says she'd like to move into larger quarters, Gretchen's thankful for the beauty surrounding her, even if it is all wet. There's a marvelous place to jog, tennis courts are nearby, and Steve has a short drive to school. "But," she says, "discipline is a little hard on the boat because space is so tight. I'm trying to balance my time between Steve and my tennis and trying to be a decent housewife and keep things nice. It's been hard, I'll admit, and it was definitely a lot simpler when I wasn't married.

"My discipline comes in trying to use my time wisely, spending enough time with him and yet practicing and playing enough tennis to be competitive. I think it would strain our relationship if I spent too much time playing tennis, because tennis isn't everything." Gretchen, who had her best professional season to date in 1989, enjoys her vocation, but after playing three years is weighing the sacrifices.

"To be super, super successful you have to be really single-minded, and I don't think I've ever had that desire to be number one or number ten or whatever. I think I've had more of a desire to be well-rounded and to be a good person with healthy relationships.

"Even that's been difficult because I travel so much and when I come home I want to be with Steve. It's hard to plan times to get together and build friendships because everyone here seems to have such busy lifestyles," she says, noting that she misses the "Howdy, y'all" friendliness of Texans. "And it takes such discipline for me to get out on the practice courts or be disciplined with my eating and sleeping. My desire to train, like with lifting weights or running, is not like it was in college or even before that when I was trying to break into the college scene. I won't say I've peaked yet but I am trying to save my knees because such a big part of my game is the strength in my legs. They're only going to last a certain amount of time!"

Living at the marina isn't exactly like growing up in Mount Lebanon, Pennsylvania, where Gretchen was the middle child of five. First, there are only a few full-time residents. And second, there are few families because parents can't exactly tell the kids to go out and play—unless they have on their swimsuits and water wings!

While in San Diego, Gretchen and Steve are attending a large church of several thousand but would like to find a smaller community church. Home fellowship groups are available but with Steve's evening classes and Gretchen's tournaments, they often find it difficult to go. Gretchen is able to meet infrequently with other believers on the circuit but with the differing match and practice schedules, even that's difficult. She mentions a close friend with whom she was able to have lunch at one tournament.

It was fun just being with her and being buddies without a lot of people around. Part of the sacrifice you have to make as a professional tennis player is not having that consistent fellowship and being in a church. A lot of times I don't want to continue to play because of that. I'd really like for us to buy a house and get into a community.

It's terribly lonely traveling and competing. But there's loneliness and then there's isolation. God can use our loneliness to draw us to Himself and not have us depend on friends or church or fellowship groups or our self-identity. Sometimes when our needs are met by all those things we can lull ourselves into thinking everything is all right with the Lord when we really need to have Him first in our lives. I sometimes lose that kind of focus when I tell people all about the great places I'm going and build it up and make it sound so neat. In tennis you always have "next week" to look forward to when you've lost badly or are feeling lonely or upset.

But like everyone else I have to discipline myself to read the Bible and pray every morning and try to share what I'm learning with Steve. I have to initiate spending time with the Lord rather than wait for others to suggest it.

For instance, I have a great friend in Texas that I called when I was visiting there, but then I started feeling bad that I don't have a friend like that around here who could encourage me like she did. But that's just where I am right now. You need those close trusting relationships, but you also need to keep your focus on God's meeting your needs. I know when I quit playing on the tennis circuit, it's going to be different.

Gretchen attended church regularly as a child with her parents, Philip and Kay Rush, and siblings back in Mount Lebanon. "I think I believed everything, but the church I was in didn't call for a public profession of faith. I think I just incorporated being a Christian into my life little by little. Sundays we went to church and on Christmas we went to midnight mass. I wouldn't say my relationship with Christ wasn't important to me, but it wasn't like *the* most important part of my life. There were those critical times when I really depended on God."

One of those was when Gretchen's dentist father died suddenly at age fifty. Gretchen, at only sixteen, discovered through that how fragile life really is. For Gretchen it was a crucial time, dealing with losing her father and yet experiencing tennis success on a national level. At the same time, there were important decisions about college offers and personal goals. She recalls crying out in pain to God and asking Him, "Why is this happening?"

My father's dying made me really think about what I wanted out of life. I searched for a deeper meaning, because I mainly thought about God only during my crisis times. It was more of a Sunday thing to do when I wasn't at a tennis tournament or when it was convenient.

But when I went to Trinity and got involved with Young Life through my suitemate at school, having a deeper relationship with Christ intrigued me. I really wanted to be around young people and be a good role model for them and get them away from all the bad stuff they could be doing and more into the church. Young Life provides good clean fun. Its leaders were committed Christians, and seeing them, I think, really opened my eyes to the importance of a personal relationship with Christ. I knew I had to make some changes. God was there but it wasn't a vital relationship.

Before, I thought I was pretty much in control of things—like my life or tennis. But I wanted to serve God not just on weekends or at church, and to do what God wanted me to do, not necessarily what I wanted to do. Through Young Life I learned that I wanted to make a difference because I have Him in control.

I wanted to surrender to God. I can't pin it down to any particular time or place, but when I heard sermons, they began to make sense, and it was kind of like my heart was ready to hear what was being said.

If I didn't have faith in God I would bottle up my frustration or yell at the linesmen or self-destruct in other ways. Faith and hope are important—having faith that He's in charge and He's taking care of you gives you hope. Winning or losing doesn't become as important as wanting to perform for Christ. You can be competitive and still be a Christian—you don't have to let people walk all over you and take your practice court or practice balls. It's just that all your identity doesn't have to be in your sport.

Although the twenty-six-year-old plans on playing tennis a few more seasons, she implies that in the near future there will be added adjustments with Steve assuming the role as main income provider.

It's been really hard for me to deal with because I come from such a traditional family where the girls picture themselves marrying a Prince Charming who is going to take care of them. It's been really hard because in our premarital Christian counseling it was stressed that the male was the spiritual leader in the home and so many times that's equated with providing financially.

That wasn't how it was when we got married because I'd already been playing professionally for half a year. Steve was going to school and a lot of things we needed to do depended on my schedule. His time was so much more flexible that it seemed like we were always adjusting to me and I haven't been real comfortable with that. It gives me hope knowing that this arrangement isn't forever. Now, he's kind of evolving into what he wants to do, so we're getting there. We are getting to be a more conventional, "normal" couple.

He really wants me to do well in tennis and says he's here to support me and that he wants me to do my best and be happy. I know, though, that he'd love to be the professional athlete because he was an athlete too and have *me* be the student, but that's not been the case.

Steve attends her major events, including trips in 1989 to London for Wimbledon and Moscow for the first professional women's tournament in the USSR. They've tried to build their relationship through staying active, but they're not exactly going courting for pleasure, at least not on the tennis courts.

"We thought sailing would be our sport that we could do together. But he likes a little more adventure than I do!" she says, describing how Steve likes to challenge the waves and nearly tips over the boat. She jokingly adds that their sport "will probably have to be bowling or something!"

Growing up the middle child among five athletic kids—including Lisel, Brad, Erika, and Molly—Gretchen says she was motivated to excel through competing for attention. When her family latched onto the game of tennis she picked it up quickly, and winning matches early encouraged her to practice and improve.

"My family wasn't already tennis oriented," she says, "so they were learning about the game with me. I had this exceptional talent, and they didn't know how to develop it. They just followed advice they were given, which was for me to get good coaching, play lots of tournaments, and go to tennis camps."

Her father had a friend who worked for a sporting goods company, and one night when she was eleven years old, he brought home new racquets for his brood. "My parents had trouble keeping us busy because we're all very active. And my father, who was very athletic even though he didn't have a tennis background, thought we could all do this together on weekends. We all learned to play about the same time." Each sibling went on to play tennis collegiately.

Gretchen started competing the next year at age twelve, getting out of the junior high band when she purportedly started practicing tennis strokes with her clarinet. "We had to play an instrument in our school. You either had to play an instrument or take something worse—like home ec," she says, then adds thoughtfully, "Now I wish I had taken that."

A strong all-around athlete, she also played softball and basketball before pursuing tennis. "I tried all the other sports there were available," she says. "Swimming I wasn't too good at. And in track I was very slow compared to the other kids in town." Quickness, which she had, not speed, is the greater asset in tennis.

Mount Lebanon was a great place to grow up, she fondly recalls. It's about twenty-three minutes by car from downtown Pittsburgh—a city proudly promoted now as the most livable city in America, she says. Her high school had 3,000 students. But the area is known more for hot high school quarterbacks than for racquet stars. It was a big deal to display her tournament souvenirs.

"I think when I first started competing I was just there to get the T-shirt!" she jokes of early tournaments she attended. She had felt "lucky to be there" in her first national tournament, which was held in North Carolina. "My eyes got real big when I saw all the other girls coming in with their coaches—and there I was with my mom and dad," she says, laughingly adding, "and we were all going to go camping as soon as I lost!"

Gradually, she began improving and gaining confidence.

"I think my brother was real instrumental in my picking up tennis because it was the only sport that we could play together. We were pretty competitive growing up and I think the challenge of trying to beat him made it fun for me because he was bigger and stronger."

When she was a high school sophomore in 1979–1980, the teachers went on strike for four months and with national tennis rankings beckoning, Gretchen struck out for Florida and a different kind of school—Nick Bolletieri's tennis school. She returned to graduate from Mount Lebanon with honors and, with improved tennis potential, parlaying her skyrocketing national rankings into numerous athletic scholarship offers.

By 1982, Gretchen was the number one ranked junior worldwide by one tennis ranking. That year she reached the quarterfinals of the U.S. Open by beating four older players. The next year, 1983, she reached another Grand Slam event quarterfinal, that time at the French Open.

Gretchen was recruited by strong West Coast powerhouses like UCLA and Stanford, but chose Trinity because of its cozy community atmosphere and the town's tremendous interest and support. The coach had emphasized "going to school, growing, and being complete as persons, and having social lives" whereas the other schools stressed competition and getting a ranking.

Gretchen seems to have done well at both.

A former four-time all-American who was ranked number one collegiately in 1984, the 5-foot-7-inch physical education and biology major was an NCAA singles and doubles finalist in both 1984 and 1985 (losing to Stanford players Linda Gates and Patty Fendick). Each time she had beaten those players in the singles and doubles team competition but, unfortunately, lost in the individuals. As a freshman in 1983, she joined with Louise Allen to win the national collegiate doubles title. Her inspired play helped Trinity to yearly top-five rankings. The NCAAs were rewarding, and yet she calls the two-week competition the "toughest tournament I've ever played. The first couple of days you play two singles and two doubles matches. You're super-charged emotionally, and you want to play well for the team.

"And then you do the individuals. By the time you're in the quarterfinals of that you don't even care if you've won or lost; I mean, you're so tired that you just have to really *want* to win."

Gretchen has represented the United States in such international events as the 1983 Pan American games (where she won gold medals in singles and in the doubles with Allen); the World University Games in Kobe, Japan; and what she terms the highlight of her career, the 1984 Olympics in Los Angeles. She and

Andrea Leand were co-winners of the Olympic qualifying event and participated along with Andrea Jaeger and Kathleen Horvath.

"The whole Olympic experience was the most memorable thing about my tennis so far," she says, savoring her moments on the UCLA courts. "I only got to play one match—it was a long match—but that was pretty great. The people were all cheering for me." She lost to France's Catherine Tanvier. All players, whether professional or amateur, had to be under twenty-one years of age to participate. A young Steffi Graf won the gold, preceding her 1988 Golden Slam that included another gold medal from Seoul and wins in each of the four major tennis championships. Even though tennis was only an exhibition sport, the players got all the same privileges as the other athletes, including uniforms, clothes, marching in the opening ceremonies and living in the Olympic Village.

With numerous other collegiate titles under her belt, Gretchen turned professional on May 26, 1986, and has carefully advanced, improving her year-end ranking from number seventy-four, to fifty-three, to forty-one, to finally cracking the top sixteen on the Virginia Slims Tour.

"I'm finally getting to that place on the pro circuit where I feel that I'm growing up, too, and maturing to where I feel that I can play with the other competitors.

"I've been a rookie for a long time," she confesses, "like about four years!" Even though her confidence has risen, some experiences still make her feel like a rookie again.

After playing outer courts and being eliminated in Wimbledon's first or second round on her first five entries, in 1989 Gretchen made the quarterfinals, only to face second-seeded Martina Navratilova on Center Court. Reaching Wimbledon's Center Court is like reaching the Super Bowl of Tennis, only with more English class and no half-time show or fireworks.

First-time players on Center Court are especially vulnerable to pressure and self-doubt. Gretchen thought her leg muscles seemed to be "at deuce" throughout the match—in other words, they were fit to be tied. "I felt pretty good when I was playing, but when I came off the court my coach asked if I had been nervous. I had tried so hard not to be, but he told me my legs were not moving at all and that's very uncharacteristic of me. I had just thought she was too good—that it wasn't me but just how well Martina was playing!

"With the history of the whole thing, I was intimidated. I was nervous and it wasn't very fun to lose," she recalls about playing on tennis's most hallowed ground. "It was a difficult situation for me to play for the first time there, especially against one of the best grass court players ever."

Even though she lost 6–2, 6–1 at Wimbledon, Gretchen picked up her biggest paycheck up to that point and valuable Virginia Slims points which later propelled her into the season-ending, million-dollar Virginia Slims World Championships in New York City. Only the top sixteen singles players and top eight doubles players qualify for the one women's event that features best-of-five-sets finals. In 1989, the November Madison Square Garden tournament would set attendance records with over a hundred thousand spectators viewing the week-long classic.

Gretchen says, most of the time it's hard to remain motivated in the fall after the Grand Slam events conclude. But when she arrived home to stacks of mail and a letter from the Women's International Tennis Association stating she might qualify for the Virginia Slims World Championships, "it really motivated me to keep going and keep playing, because it would have been easy to stop after Wimbledon—that was such a great thing. I just never thought I would be able to qualify for the Slims tournament in singles. Then when Chris Evert retired it opened up another spot."

After losing in the second round of the U.S. Open to Czechoslovakia's Helena Sukova, Gretchen entered the Soviet Union's first women's professional tennis tournament in early October. Snow had already fallen in Moscow and yet even when the weather turned cold and rainy outside, it didn't deter her warmth and enthusiasm for the Moscow Open inside. Gretchen and Steve went over several days early to sightsee and "did a lot of looking around" then and during their ten-day stay.

Although initially apprehensive because, as she jokingly says, she'd seen too many spy movies,

> We found out that the people were just so happy to have us there. They were really curious about America and they wanted our jeans and tennis shoes—anything that was Western.
>
> It's terribly exciting now to see what's going on there. You feel like you're a part of it because you've been there and you can relate to the people. Many wanted to come and practice their English on us.
>
> They were really excited about having their first professional tournament.

Spectators treated each match as though it were Wimbledon East, cheering enthusiastically with each rally. Although Pam Shriver was top-seeded, Gretchen won the $100,000 tournament over the thirty-two-player field, beating Russians Larisa Savchenko in the semifinals and Natalia Zvereva in the finals. That tournament win solidified her chances of making the Slims Finals, but still it would be necessary to out-point her challengers at the Virginia Slims of Chicago tournament.

"It was a pretty large tournament with $300,000 in prize money, and when I saw the other girls had easier draws, I wasn't so sure I could qualify. There were actually four or five players vying for that last spot and I got a pretty rough draw, meeting a seeded player in the first round." Gretchen's first-round opponent, Mary Joe Fernandez, already had qualified for the Slims Championships by being ranked in the top ten.

Gretchen upset the higher-ranked player and earned more computer ranking points during that tournament than her rivals, thus qualifying her for the New York field. Even though Gretchen lost to Argentine defending champion Gabriela Sabatini in the first round in New York, making the Championships was a bonus. "I felt lucky to be there," she says. "It was a special treat."

So was returning to the *Gypsy Lady*. There's plenty of smooth sailing ahead for this young athlete.

# 11

# *Debbie Brown*

## Serving her country

THE LETTER APPEARED in the February 1980 sports section of the *Los Angeles Times*:

Dear Editor,

It's really hard for me to read the things so many people are saying today regarding the athletes' reaction to the Olympic boycott. They are being called unpatriotic and selfish and many other unfair things. I can tell you from being around my daughter and the national volleyball team that these are some of the most patriotic people that you will ever come across today.

My daughter Debra has worked extremely exhausting hours developing her skills, body strength and endurance, as well as her mental alertness and toughness. She has sacrificed most of the social events that her peers were enjoying while she worked out after school and evenings. She postponed her education to devote full time to her sport. She spent many months in foreign lands studying their techniques. She and her teammates experienced many losses and few wins at first, but persistently improved. The United States has a group of young women who can match or beat any volleyball team in the world.

I can speak for most of these women, especially Debra, when I say their pride in representing our country is much more or at least equal to their own personal reasons.

I know how inspired Debra was when an older Olympic athlete told her what a fantastic experience it was to represent his country in the Olympics. She has mentioned it many times since, and has told me how she always has that sense of pride when representing the United States in international competition; how she always gets goose bumps when she hears the national anthem being played.

Our athletes have chosen goals of their own free wills. They are not coerced. They are not regimented. This is what they want to show the world, as well as their intelligence, personal character, and highly skilled athletic abilities.

Charles C. Landreth
El Segundo

The normally soft-spoken Charlie, father of five and a house painter by trade in this beach city near Los Angeles International Airport, wanted to counter the overwhelming criticism he had read too frequently on the opinion pages. No one could understand the sacrifice and struggle that athletes like his daughter, Debbie, co-captain of the U.S. women's volleyball team, had made, he wrote. And then for them to be denied the opportunity to compete by circumstances out of their control, well, that just didn't seem fair.

President Jimmy Carter's decision denying U.S. athletes a trip to Moscow for the XXII Olympiad affected many. The American sports fans were torn. After all, other boycotts had been attempted, such as the grain embargo against the Soviets. Even the Olympics had been touched in 1976 by the African nations' walkout. But in this boycott, American athletes were the innocent pawns.

While their rivals competed for Olympic medals, young Americans nursed their disappointment, accepting commemorative medals in Washington, D.C., from Congress and the United States Olympic Committee. Before the American athletes stepped forward individually on the morning of July 30, 1980, to receive their medals from USOC officials, Carter addressed the assemblage.

If our Olympic team had been in Moscow these past days, with all the pageantry and spectacle, it would have been impossible for us to credibly maintain our continuing effort to seek freedom in Afghanistan. No matter what else we had done, no matter what other steps we had taken, our participation would have sent an unmistakable message—to the Soviet government, to the Soviet people, and the people all over the world. That message would have been like this: The United States may not like the idea of aggression, but when it comes down to it, we are willing to join the parade as if nothing had happened. For the sake of world peace, we cannot allow such a message to be conveyed.[1]

---

1. *The Olympian* vol. 7, no. 3 (September 1980): 5.

The president met later with the Olympians at a White House lawn reception and told them he was honored to shake their hands. "You have done more to uphold the Olympic ideal than any other group of athletes in American history," he said as he thanked them for their sacrifice.[2]

They were named Olympians, but the Olympic creed, "Not the winning, but the taking part," was not to be fulfilled. The torch would be passed to a new generation. Athletes like Debbie lost out.

Soon after the Soviets invaded Afghanistan on December 26, 1979, rumors had circulated that the United States government would retaliate by keeping its athletes home and preventing American broadcasters from financing Moscow's Olympic competition through paid television rights. The rumors were distracting, but in women's volleyball, the team trained on.

"It was pretty tough to keep your mind on the right kinds of things. There was a chance we would go. We were one of the best in the world by then," says Debbie today, recalling that even though they had finished fifth in their last major tournament before the Olympics (the 1978 World Championships), they had beaten every top team, including the Chinese, Japanese, and Soviets, and had qualified for the 1980 Olympics out of the NORCECA (North America, Caribbean, and Central America) zone second behind powerful world-champion Cuba.

The official announcement came while Deb and her teammates, including Flo Hyman, Debbie Green, co-captain Patti Dowdell, Terry Place, Sue Woodstra, Coach Arie Selinger, and others, were touring the United States with the East German national team and whitewashing them 3–0 each night. They were returning to their San Antonio, Texas, hotel rooms for a meeting when Selinger broke the difficult news.

> The only team we had not beaten and that I think we probably feared a little was Cuba, and yet in 1980 they didn't even win a medal. And it was doubly disappointing to not compete because the East Germans won the silver [behind the Soviets] and we had beaten them every match that spring.
>
> Arie didn't want to believe it. He was always real optimistic even up to the time the USOC was deciding. He kept saying, "There's a 99 percent chance we will get to go. I just know it." A lot of the girls really hung on this hope, and it was tough because I didn't really

2. Ibid.

believe it. I really didn't think we were going to go. But I said if there was a 1 percent chance, I would hang in there. Actually, when we got the news it wasn't like this big blow that I just couldn't believe, because it had been building for months.

The months between the time a boycott was suggested and when it was actually announced were tough because Debbie's teammates would come to her as team captain and ask probing questions. Debbie doubted that they'd go, and encouraged her friends to accept whatever the outcome was. "We're just going to have to live with it. When we find out, then we can deal with it," she told them.

"Most of the time, Arie and I got along really well, but he wanted me to tell the team that we *were* going to go, and I just couldn't do that. I couldn't sit there and tell them that," Debbie recalls.

Following the Winter Olympics in Lake Placid, New York, Debbie and representatives of other Olympic teams were invited to the White House to meet with Carter on the Afghanistan crisis and its relation to the Summer Olympic Games. Debbie thought the March 21 meeting would be a forum for discussing the possibility of a boycott; instead, she and the other representatives got a history and geography lesson from the president's advisers, including Zbigniew Brzezinski and Lloyd Cutler. They described the invasion and said that the president would be out shortly to tell them why they were not going to the Olympics. The news hit like Hurricane Hugo.

"I can remember the speculation after the Winter Olympics thinking that the success of the hockey team would shut down that thinking about a boycott. It was kind of a hope that the athletes had, but when we got to the White House it was just blown away," Debbie says.

The president stated that the government had talked to other countries, including Japan, China, and Great Britain and that all were unsure about participating, but that he was absolutely sure that the United States would not go. "That was what he came out and said. It wasn't like it was a great discussion. He just said that it doesn't matter what the other countries do because we're not going. He made that political statement and that was it. It was really something that was hard to grasp, but the hardest thing during that time was reading the opinion pages of the newspapers."

The volleyballers would check the newspapers daily for the latest information, and couldn't avoid seeing the public's criticism of the athletes who said they still wanted to participate. Debbie recalls,

A lot of people started jumping on the athletes, saying we would show the Soviet Union and we shouldn't send our athletes; that the boycott was great. All these letters said the boycott was right and wondered how the athletes could be so selfish as to want to compete in the Moscow Games—like all the athletes think about is competing and they don't know what's going on in the world.

It was hard to read that stuff and realize that was what the general public thought. That's when I started thinking, "Hey, if that's what the general public thinks and they're the ones who send us, then I guess we shouldn't go. If that's the way it is, then maybe they're right." It was real hard. That's when my dad wrote the letter.

Mr. Landreth also wrote that the athletes felt that an Olympic boycott alone was the least effective measure, but perhaps would be more effective if coupled with other penalties.

The letter clearly expressed Charlie's feelings, but the general public could still never know the athletes' struggles.

The youngest in a family of five, including sisters ten and eleven years older and brothers one and five years older, Debbie had always been competitive on the playground and playing sports channeled that energy.

"I pushed myself. I really wanted to win, in running or relay races or any stupid little thing," she says now, recalling that she could even beat the boys. "I really didn't care who I was going against. We had a pretty neat neighborhood with a lot of kids who were pretty active. Maybe it was Southern California and being outside all the time," she says. "I was always asking my dad if I could go out and play, too."

Debbie's neighborhood produced other professional athletes like Keebler produces cookies: George Brett of the Kansas City Royals and his brother Ken; Scott MacGregor, formerly of the Baltimore Orioles; and Keith Erickson, the UCLA grad who starred with the Los Angeles Lakers. Debbie added to the pride of El Segundo in the fall of 1989, when her portrait likewise was displayed in the El Segundo Hall of Fame at the high school.

Going "out to play" might mean retrieving baseballs that Charlie, a frequent youth league coach, hit to her older brothers. "I thought I could do anything my brothers could do. Mostly I just wanted my dad to spend some time with me and throw me some balls or let me run around the bases," she says. Little sister hung around enough to absorb some skills, later helping her Bobby Sox teams to two national titles in Buena Park, California. Though her brothers had started Little League much younger, softball was the first organized sport Debbie played, beginning in the fifth grade. Her dad's athletic interests motivated her to learn quickly, and he taught her to play to the best of her ability.

He was always in real great shape, even though he didn't work out or anything. He was naturally strong from the physical labor of house painting. I can remember when he turned fifty and I was playing softball, some parents and friends asked how old he was. They couldn't believe it because he was in such great shape. And he *was!* Even his stomach was rock hard.

The Landreths resembled other sixties families portrayed on TV shows like "Leave it to Beaver" and "Ozzie and Harriet." Dad had time for the kids and being Mom meant twenty-four-hour duty. Debbie's mother, Dorothy, stayed home until Debbie was in the sixth grade before taking a job as a part-time teller in a bank down the street, then advancing to become branch operations officer.

"Until now, I guess I didn't realize how important it was to have Mom around all the time," Debbie says. "When I came home from school, she was always there with snacks and a listening ear. By the time I was in sixth grade I was pretty responsible, and if I did need her she was just down the street."

Debbie's experience in volleyball began when some of her freshman high school friends who had played the sport in parochial school convinced her to go out for the team. Softball was the only other "girls'" sport offered then, and her introduction to volleyball wasn't thrilling, she says.

"I went out for the volleyball team not knowing anything about it, and I really didn't like it. I had some close friends that were already playing volleyball and they were pretty good. I went out for it because of them. They said it would be fun and I wanted to stay busy." Later, volleyball would turn into more than busywork; for Debbie it produced opportunities that would lead to a career.

Debbie recalls that her first coach was a great lady, but not very knowledgeable about volleyball. The next year the girls got a new coach, an enthusiastic UCLA graduate named Barb Bernlohr. "It was a tremendous difference when Barb came. We thought she was great and she was!" Debbie says. Between Debbie's sophomore and junior years Barb got nearly the whole team to go to a big regional United States Volleyball Association camp. It was outdoors with nearly twenty grass courts on which to play. Bernlohr attended the coaches' camp to improve her coaching skills.

After Deb's junior year, the team's mainstays graduated, leaving Debbie to attend the camp by herself. Barb's coaching helped her improve, but Debbie recalls that Barb's greatest lesson was her personal interest and concern for her athletes. "She wanted each of us to grow as a person as well as an athlete. She just gave of herself a lot. I think that had more impact on me overall than whatever she was telling me on the court."

The coach demonstrated that kind of concern when she drove Debbie up to the 1973 summer volleyball camp an hour north in Carpinteria. For Debbie, the trip itself was memorable. Barb's car was decorated with "Jesus First" bumper stickers and as drivers would pass, they would give the "One Way" to heaven sign, pointing skyward with index finger extended. Barb would respond excitedly, and the drivers would honk. Debbie would sink lower in the front seat.

"I knew she was a Christian but at that point we thought Christians who were real vocal about it were "Jesus freaks." I loved her and I thought she was great, but you know, in our little circle we kind of made fun of her and stuff because of that. There we were on the freeways of Los Angeles and people were honking at us and it was so strange," Debbie recalls, demonstrating how she slouched in the front seat, embarrassed and trying to hide because to her Christianity was so uncool.

To Debbie, Christianity was a social thing of attending church and youth group, void of any spiritual aspects. Her spiritual needs were diverted socially in a religious organization for girls that emphasized achieving different levels of elective offices before finally arriving at the top position of being the honored queen. For achievement-oriented Debbie, the two-and-a-half-year process was too time consuming, but she did learn to apply the group's watchword, "Let it be a lesson to each one of us to be thoughtful before we speak."

"I have never, never forgotten that, since I used to say it every week." Because of Barb, her coach, and the girls' organization, Debbie's curiosity about spiritual matters deepened.

The four-year volleyball starter and female athlete of the year graduated in 1974 and then attended a local community college.

She also played for a Southern California junior club volleyball team sponsored by the sport shoe company, Adidas, coached by Chuck Erbe. She traveled to Canada and Mexico competing with the junior national team, composed mostly of Adidas players, before spending six weeks training in South Korea.

That experience was difficult, but the teenager persevered through her first extended overseas trip. "It was one of the toughest things I've ever been through—being away from home for six weeks and doing nothing but training," she says. The athletes lived at the Seoul Foreign School with cots set up in the hallway and only one shower available. Cultural differences, food, and isolation were unfamiliar obstacles to the young athletes. "There was not a day that went by that somebody wasn't crying for some reason or other; either because Chuck got on to them about something or just from being homesick." The stress was formidable, yet it molded the future nucleus of the women's volleyball national team, including Debbie Green, Carolyn Becker, Sue Woodstra, and Terry Place. Shared suffering makes for tight relationships.

Volleyball, a cousin to another indoor sport—basketball, has increased greatly in popularity since its inception in Holyoke, Massachusetts in 1895. Czechoslovakia hosted the first World Championships in 1949 and volleyball became an Olympic sport in 1964 in Tokyo.

Cuba became the dominant NORCECA power and the hastily formed U.S. all-start teams couldn't beat them and couldn't qualify for major tournaments. A month's practice before an event couldn't beat countries which maintained year-round competitive national teams. America's typical international finishes included the women's twelfth-place showing in the 1974 World Championships and the men's nineteenth-place effort in 1978. And Americans had qualified for only one Olympiad, Mexico City in 1968.

Only eight teams qualify for Olympic competition: a winner of each of the five geographical zones, the defending Olympic champion, the world champion, and the host country. Sometimes teams can enter through a prequalifying tournament and in 1976, though they had improved greatly, the U.S. women lost a heartbreaker final to East Germany. The East Germans went to Montreal, the Americans stayed home. Yet Debbie sensed there might be a breakthrough if the team nucleus stayed together.

Enrolling at the University of Southern California, Debbie led the Trojan women to two national collegiate titles in 1976 and 1977 while the team compiled a 72–1 record. The 5-foot-8-inch outside hitter earned first team all-American honors both years, capped by the Mikasa Award as the country's best all-around player.

Off the court, she explored her spiritual interests in some religion classes, but it would take the example of a boyfriend and a simple explanation from a junior varsity volleyball team member to point her toward Christianity.

Debbie, the Associated Student Body vice-president at El Segundo High School had been dating her friend Steve, the popular ASB president, for five years when she began receiving curious letters from him. Debbie, then spending the summer of 1977 in Pasadena, Texas, with the national team, read that Steve had become a born-again Christian and she didn't know what to think.

> I remember getting some letters and thinking Steve had flipped out. It really had an impact on me, because I respected him a lot and I knew he was a rational, intelligent person. I guess I thought I didn't know any rational, intelligent people who had accepted Christ.
>
> I had always understood that if you acted like a Christian then you could be called a Christian. Mostly I was intrigued into thinking, "What's the deal here?" I wasn't willing to say he'd "lost it" because I respected him so much.

Steve gladly shared his new faith with Debbie and her family, but they were confused by his sudden religious enthusiasm. Yet Debbie's interest had been piqued. Back at USC in November of 1977, when she overheard Sharon Lehoskey, a junior varsity player, invite another teammate to discuss Christianity over lunch, Debbie wanted in on it, too.

"Sharon was real involved with Campus Crusade for Christ and I knew that I could ask her questions about Christianity or about born-again Christians if I wanted to. So I asked her, 'When are we going to lunch?'" Sharon, unintimidated about sharing Christ with a world-class volleyball player, agreed to get together the next day. After Sharon's explanation about what it meant to accept Christ, Debbie was ready to prayerfully invite Him into her life.

A few months later Debbie rejoined the national team, settling in at the new Olympic Training Center in Colorado Springs. The USVBA had decided if the United States were ever going to be competitive internationally the team would have to train together year-round instead of selecting only all-stars. The first American team to train at the facility full time, the volleyballers were surprised at the former military base's sparseness.

"We actually drove by it and were making jokes like, 'That's probably it,' and it was horrifying to discover that really was where we were going to be. We couldn't believe it." The facility was marked by only a tiny sign saying U.S. Olympic Training Center with barbed wire atop the fence.

The volleyballers stayed in individual rooms with shared bathrooms in what formerly was the officers' quarters.

Debbie recalls living in the barracks with a view into the next ugly green building. No mountain or prairie views were available. A cafeteria provided meals, and the site contained only one inadequate gym. Practices were held in local high schools, with space available from 6:00 to 8:00 A.M., plus a longer four-hour practice in the afternoon. Traveling and workouts prevented the women from holding down jobs and yet they received only an eighty dollar monthly stipend from the USVBA. It wasn't much, but it was a start. And Colorado Springs was enthusiastic about hosting them. Debbie's sisters helped by sending checks periodically for twenty or twenty-five dollars. "I'd be so thankful and think that was just unbelievable," she says.

Now U.S. volleyball has developed a national training center in San Diego, with workouts at the Federal Building in beautiful Balboa Park, home of the famous San Diego Zoo. In what would have been only a wild dream ten years ago, team members participate in the Olympic Job Opportunities Program which allows them to pursue career-related jobs locally and be paid full-time salaries for "flex-time" work. Players can earn living expenses and prepare for post-volleyball jobs while developing their athletic skills to the fullest. The concept has allowed the United States to continually recruit new talent and keep it.

Today, the players don't really have a concept of what we went through. I'm a national team coach and sometimes it's irritating to hear them complaining about how tough they have it. But I don't really talk about it with them because it would be like my parents telling me how tough they had it walking miles and miles to school. It doesn't matter and it doesn't mean anything to you. They may be interested and ask questions, but they don't have a concept of what we went through. I remember how far twenty-five dollars would go then, but now I say, "What can I do with *that?*"

Other difficulties Debbie had then included going to church since she had no personal transportation. Instead, she tried studying the Bible study materials Sharon Lehoskey provided. Gradually, Debbie began to know more about what her faith meant. Within the year, this growing faith would be severely tested by circumstances beyond her control.

Selinger, who headed the national team from 1975 until 1984, was the head coach, assisted for a short time by Erbe. The women trained hard on a full-time basis beginning in 1978 and showed quick improvement. The American athletes knew the women in all the other top volleyball countries were together year-round and had very well-developed clubs to play on between Olympics and the periods when they weren't with the national team. "We didn't even have a shot if we weren't doing something similar to that," Debbie says.

The United States advanced to fifth place in the 1978 World Championships and then qualified for the Olympics in the 1979 NORCECA championships in Cuba. But seven months later came the Soviet invasion of Afghanistan, and the controversial Olympic boycott.

They took polls all the time on what people thought and there really was a sway toward our not going. Then after the decision was made to not send the athletes, it went the other way. People started saying we ought to be there and this isn't right, this isn't going to change a thing. And the public went completely the other way and we had tremendous support.

I could say, well, we learned it didn't do any good. Looking back, I would think a politician would think the same thing: that it did not accomplish what it set out to accomplish so that basically it needlessly hurt a lot of people. It denied people something they had worked pretty hard at. I would hope that it would never happen again. I think it has really set a precedent that's been pretty damaging to athletics.

Looking back, Debbie is not bitter, although she easily could be, having invested seven years of her life pursuing a goal, only to have it disappear through circumstances outside her control. Yet she says,

I did everything in my power to reach my goal. I have to be able to accept it. I knew I had a choice to be bitter and feel sorry for myself or pick myself up and get on with life—make the best of it or be miserable. Circumstances can make you bitter or better, depending on your response. It wasn't until later that I could understand and believe God was in control through all this. If it had been God's will, I would have been there.

Debbie had prepared for a coaching career after her playing days; the boycott shortened her appearances in the U.S. team uniform by a few months. Coach Selinger had convinced most of Debbie's teammates to stay, at least through the 1982 World Championships. After finishing third there, an Olympic medal seemed possible in two years in Los Angeles and many decided to keep playing. Ranked first or second worldwide in the early eighties, the team finally got its chance as the host team, and the young women were rewarded with Olympic silver medals.

But at age twenty-three, after having been selected USVBA all-American eight times and playing in two World Championships, one Pan American Games, and one World University Games, Debbie was ready to get on with life. Debbie accepted an assistant coach position at Arizona State University where she finished her degree in physical education.

By this time, she also had met a certain Colorado Springs sportswriter named Dennis Brown and their relationship was blossoming. Dennis had covered the team's journey to Cuba for the 1979 NORCECA Olympic qualifying tournament.

Not long after they had started dating Debbie noticed a Bible among Dennis's books. Peeking inside, she was surprised at how various passages were underlined and how he had written notes inside as though it were a college textbook. Feeling that she was intruding on personal thoughts, she had shut it quickly.

Even though Dennis had been actively involved in a Young Life group in high school, the couple hadn't yet discussed the importance of their Christian faith in their relationship. That innocent foray into Dennis's Bible opened doors to deeper communication. "Finally, when we became engaged, it was something important to us. Our lives changed tremendously. We've tried to base our marriage on what the Bible says," Debbie confides today.

Dennis followed Debbie to the Phoenix area, taking a job with the *Phoenix Gazette,* and the two got married in 1981. Debbie continued coaching at ASU, moving up to head coach in 1983, and compiling a 106–82 record in six years while leading the Sun Devils into five National Collegiate Athletic Association tournaments. Terry Liskevych, currently the U.S. women's head coach, recruited her as a part-time assistant in 1987, and after taking a leave of absence from ASU, she reported full time in 1989.

Debbie remains as positive today as ever, pursuing coaching wholeheartedly.

> I knew how a coach could positively influence someone's life. I pretty much had positive influences from coaches and I guess I really appreciated it and thought it would be something that I would like to be able to do—to give to kids the way coaches gave to me.
>
> My dad was a great example. He was so patient with me. I had a real temper, and my parents must have just pulled their hair out sometimes trying to think how they could control this unruly child. I sure wasn't one of those kids the coaches say was great to work with. I worked hard, but coachability wasn't one of my greatest assets. I was competitive and I didn't quit. And you couldn't work me hard enough. But I had that temper.

Telling about the time she angrily kicked a ball off the gym wall, Debbie says,

> Chuck Erbe, my former coach, had a pretty important impact on me, teaching me that some types of behavior are acceptable and some are not. He yelled at me loud enough that you could hear it everywhere: "That does not happen in my gym, and it will not happen again!" I respected him and I knew that he was a good coach; and I wanted to learn from him. I had people like that all along the way who told me the right things at the right time.

Debbie applied enough of what she learned from that kind of good coaching to establish herself as one of the premier players in the game during the seventies. She plans to apply those same principles now as a coach. While she recognizes many factors are different today from when she grew up in El Segundo, and despite the prestige and satisfaction of being an assistant coach for the women's national volleyball team, she believes that it's important for her to be with their kids, should she and Dennis have children. And she definitely keeps her relationship with Dennis a top priority.

> If I had children, I would want to be there and raise them. I think it's good for them to be around other children, but I firmly believe if you're going to make the commitment to have children, then raising them is a pretty big responsibility. I don't think I would have the problem of finding motherhood boring or thinking what will I do with myself?

Coaching the national team wouldn't be all that hard to give up—it's not as glamorous as people think it is. It's a great opportunity to get out and see the world and if Dennis could go with me on every trip, then I might reconsider. It's hard for me when the team leaves for extended periods of time. I don't enjoy that part of it. If it were something we were doing *together* then I might say, "Wow, this is great! I might miss this."

In 1988, we both took a leave of absence from January until October after the Olympics, and it was like we were on "play time"! Next time we go to Europe for a tournament, we've talked about meeting toward the end of the tournament and taking a week or two of actual vacation instead of just being in a gym and watching volleyball. He loves watching the team and he's a great fan, but it would be fun to have that time *and* a *real* vacation!

For Debbie Brown, improving her serve means more than perfecting a volleyball skill. It means serving her husband, her country, and most of all the Lord Jesus Christ.

# 12

# *Nancy Swider-Peltz*

## Coming back . . .
## and back . . . and back

WHETHER GLIDING THROUGH it swimming or sliding on top of it skating, Nancy Swider-Peltz is the consummate water baby. From swimming strokes to skating strokes: what will she take up next? Rowing? Stroke, stroke, stroke? Or golf, where you don't want strokes? Painting—with brush strokes? Or triathlon, where you practically suffer a stroke.

A five-time NCAA Division III all-American swimmer at Wheaton College in Illinois, Nancy traded a one-piece Spandex swimsuit for a one-piece Spandex hooded track suit and in the process earned a position on four United States Olympic speed-skating teams: 1976 (Innsbruck), 1980 (Lake Placid), 1984 (Sarajevo), and 1988 (Calgary). Twice she's set world records: in 1976 in Inzell, West Germany (3,000 meters) and in 1980 in Savalen, Norway (10,000 meters). Nancy comments,

> Having modest success has given me the self-confidence of having accomplished goals that I set. That's very important in life. Not that I've totally reached the gold-medal goal, but just making the attempt and dealing with the obstacles gives you a certain confidence that you can handle things; that the training I've gone through in this sport to make the Olympic teams makes me believe that nothing else is going to be more difficult in living each day. Life is not going to be that tough in comparison. I think you become mentally tough and more able to handle your ups and downs.

Today, with a baby (Jeffrey, Jr., born in July 1989) and a toddler (Nancy, born in January 1987) at home, she needs that mental

128

toughness. Little kids can challenge the creativity and confidence of almost anyone. Sometimes, Nancy knows, it's hard to even put two thoughts together.

In 1987, at thirty-one, an age when many mothers would be plotting what to make their kids for dinner, she was planning dinner *and* plotting a comeback in the speed-skating arena.

After she married former Wheaton College football player Jeff Peltz in May of 1985, Nancy gradually opted for more coaching and less skating. She hyphenated her name, Swider-Peltz, to honor her father. Only a year later Nancy was surprised to find herself pregnant and thought her career was over. Not that the little child wasn't important; she was—and is—a blessing, Nancy says. It was just that Nancy had hoped to leave open her options to continue skating a while longer. She even told fellow Olympian Dan Jansen that she wouldn't skate again, even for a million dollars. "And if I did, I'd pay him the million dollars," Nancy says. "He's still trying to collect!

"I honestly believed after the 1984 Olympics that that might be it for me in skating. But you just never know. And when I found out I was pregnant, I was upset and crying, thinking that I wouldn't ever skate in competition again," the 5-foot-6-inch dynamo says. "But I knew I hadn't reached my potential yet."

Little Nancy was born January 10, 1987, after a difficult labor and a Caesarean delivery. Just six weeks later the new mother managed some light running—make that a fast walk—but it wasn't until a family outing on July fourth that the pain during exercise began to subside.

Nancy was at a traditional family get-together at the home of her parents, John, Sr., and Delores, in Park Ridge, Illinois. Nancy calls her mom "energetic and fun-loving. She wants to be in on all the recreational activities, not just watch. She's the type who'll be out there building sand castles and running with the kids." Nancy says her dad is loving but purposeful, a dad who didn't withhold compliments but reserved them for special occasions, so "he really meant it." At a Swider clan gathering there are lots of games, from throwing footballs to throwing darts to, of course, the Famous Swider Mile. Pressure is always on each participant to, as Nancy says, "bust their guts!"

"It's fun, but everybody takes it pretty seriously," says Nancy, whose older brothers John, Jr., and Mike both played football at Wheaton. Mike is now an associate head coach at Wheaton, under J. R. Bishop, while John, Jr., is dean of students at a local high school. All three siblings have homes within a half-mile of each other.

"I ran and I felt decent and it was the first time the C-section didn't hurt when I ran. I ran under a 6-minute mile and it didn't hurt later either, so I started training for a triathlon. I couldn't believe it felt so good to be working out again," she remarks. By August, Nancy had competed in the Crystal Lake Triathlon—swimming, biking, and running to second place. Now she began contemplating another skating comeback. "I said if I could get a sponsor, I would try. I was quite surprised to be able to get some control back in my training."

Nancy's father, a football and swimming coach in the Chicago school system, retired early to assist her. She had only three months to train for the Olympic trials in December. That meant frequently flying with her dad to Calgary to work out indoors, as well as paying for skates, training gear, ice time, and coaching. She says husband Jeff was hesitant—he knew she had the ability—but he wasn't sure if they could juggle family responsibilities and finances *and* find the work-out time required.

While looking for sponsors, Nancy unexpectedly met a friend who worked for Kemper Financial, a Fortune 500 company in Chicago, and communicated her need for support so that she could train full time. "He knew I was a dedicated skater and he sold the company on it. We wrapped it up within four days. They gave me a jacket and I made a headband with their logo and they really didn't expect anything from me in return, but I always try to share my appreciation for their assistance when I speak."

After winning five gold medals in 1980, the fabulous Eric Heiden retired at age twenty-one. Most skaters retire within a few years of that age, Nancy mentions. And yet here Nancy was trying an unprecedented comeback. Maybe the Russians, with their state support, or the Dutch, whose national sport is skating, could continue past that age—but certainly not an American woman. And a new mother, no less. Who would even *want* to go back to the bitter cold when you could toast your toes in front of a warm fireplace? In the sport of speed skating, being thirty-one makes you a veritable senior citizen, and Nancy would be the oldest on the American squad.

> I think speed skating weeds out those people who want to take things easy. To make it you've got to accept the fact that it's hard work with little or no glory. You'll probably never make a career of it.

And it's going to be cold. It's going to be *very* cold. It's going to be cold day after day—and you can't just take time off and wait for good weather. When the wind chill is 60 degrees below zero and you're trying to keep your muscles warm and your attitude up, it weeds out anybody who at all wants to be comfortable.

Also, there is a lot of travel; you might possibly have to drop out of school and have your parents support you; and it's not glorious like, say, gymnastics which is televised and has a lot of fan support. Or even high school football, which a lot of boys go out for because it's going to be glorious. Speed skating isn't.

Speed skating is a sport for the hard workers. Oh, sure, improvements have come: sleek, hooded, wind-resistant, fitted racing suits; adjustable blades; huge indoor rinks; the measuring of lactate levels (which might indicate overtraining). But nothing can replace competitive desire as an asset. If a research scientist could discover and isolate *that* variable, and then bottle it and sell it, it would make him or her rich.

There are many challenging factors about speed skating, yet all have drawn Nancy deeper into the sport. When she was young it was simply that she loved going fast. Now, she knows that through diligence she can be successful in competition.

While preparing for the 1976 Olympic Trials she labored through her brothers' football drills to build her endurance, leg strength, and mental toughness. "To me, training myself was just a sign that if you worked hard enough at that time you could get close to the top in skating," she notes. Ignorant then about tapering training prior to a big event, she still managed to come in seventh in the 3000-meter race. Only five weeks later, after laying off following the Olympics, Nancy set a world record in the event.

"I trained in 1976 with the goal of beating the Russians, who were the best in the world," she remembers, comparing that dream to Olympic wrestler Dan Gable's (now the national coach), who wrestled Russians continually in his mind. "My goal was to make an Olympic team, go for a medal, and go back to school and graduate with my class. I just believed that if I was going to win a medal, I had to train more strenuously than the rest of the Americans."

Prior to 1976, the Americans didn't train hard enough to consistently win in international competition; afterwards, Nancy says, they trained too hard. "There are enough people in this world who will train hard; it's who will train smart. You've got to know when to rest, when to train, when to do sprint work, when to do endurance work, when to compete, when to back off, when you're about to overtrain. I think between 1976 and 1980 the U.S. speed-skating team trained so hard many of them burned out."

Looking back, Nancy feels that 1976 would have been her best chance at winning a medal when hard work alone could reap benefits. Even in the off-season she persevered.

> In the summer you have to work to keep your mental attitude up with all the training—no ice means no competition. You've got to bike, run hills, do the slide board. (You put socks on over your shoes and slide back and forth in simulated skating with a sideward, not forward, motion.) Even when you're putting in all that work you have to realize you might be a great summer trainer and not be able to skate worth anything or vice versa; you might not train hard and still be a great skater.

> It's a problem recruiting people into the sport because the only reward is the individual's personal satisfaction at accomplishing something. You don't go into this sport thinking you're going to make a lot of money. Now, money is starting to come in from the United States Olympic Committee, but you still have to be on the national team to receive any. But even that is so much better than what I ever received. I mean, I missed it all.

Well, maybe not quite. It's not every speed skater who perseveres enough to earn national team spots in four Olympiads, graduate from college, get married, and have a child.

In December 1987 Nancy qualified in West Allis, Wisconsin, for her fourth Olympic team. She competed in Calgary in the 1000-meters and also the 5000-meters. Nancy was awed by the indoor skating facility and the opportunity to skate under ideal conditions. There are other such indoor facilities (Holland, Norway, East Germany), she says, adding that Calgary was the first and most impressive.

"It's unbelievable! That was the enticement for me, coming back in 1988. I just couldn't believe how fun it was to be able to skate and not have to deal with wind or rain or unfair conditions," she says. With such grand facilities, perhaps skating will increase in popularity as basketball did when it came in out of the rain—it had been played outdoors until the late 1930s.

After a fortnight in Canada the winter Olympians were invited to visit President Ronald Reagan at the White House. By that time little Nancy was thirteen months old, so she sat on her mother's lap during the lengthy ceremonies. White House officials informed the pair that if there were any problems, both would have to leave. Afterward, the athletes in each sport were invited to have a group picture taken with the president, after first being informed about such security rules as not handing anything to the president. When it was the speed-skating team's turn and President Reagan noticed her baby girl, Nancy asked the president to hold her daughter. He graciously consented despite the security guards' consternation, and Nancy excitedly handed her over to the president!

"Well," said Reagan in typical fashion, "I haven't done this in a while!" Nancy, along with the other skaters including Dan Jansen and Bonnie Blair, posed for a group shot with the president holding little Nancy. That picture hangs now on a wall in Nancy's home.

The athlete has stored her slide board in the garage—for now— where the dust bunnies gather on those kinds of things that most garages of families with young children seem to attract—play pens, baby swings, and toys—lots of toys. Somehow, there's space for a car.

Nancy's ranch-style home is decorated in popular country blue and dusty rose. She's sewn the drapes and many of the decorative sofa pillows herself. On the wall, dedicated to the "ice princess," there's a carved plaque noting Nancy's speed-skating accomplishments. It's a short jog to 2200-student Wheaton College, home of the Billy Graham Evangelistic Center.

Nancy grew up practically in the back yard of O'Hare International Airport. At age twelve she joined a Park Ridge skating club coached by Richard Wellbank. At first she'd enter "kiddie" events like races sponsored by the local Junior Chamber of Commerce. In the summers she'd swim.

At Maine South High School she ran track (her mile relay team won the state title and broke a national record) and swam varsity four years (she finished second in the state in the 100-yard breaststroke). But life was more than sports. Her parents wanted her to be well-rounded so they started her in violin lessons during grammar school. "I would have loved to have been better," she says now about playing a musical instrument. "I always watch the violinists during concerts. But I just didn't have time to practice." Her parents didn't have enough money for private lessons, either, so her violin playing ended up second fiddle to skating.

During high school she was a cheerleader four years (captain twice), attended the Illinois Girls' State (which simulates government in action), played in the concert orchestra four years, and was the second runner-up in the Junior Miss Contest in 1973. She rode a unicycle for the talent section. She graduated in 1974 as the school's outstanding female athlete.

Her family has always been close. Nancy credits her parents for that and for their hand in her skating ventures. "If it weren't for my parents I would never have been able to do what I did, because they supported me financially as well as being there to watch me at competitions."

She attended church as a youngster, and learned Bible verses, and she recalls praying at age six with Mike, all of a year older, to accept Jesus Christ. When her training intensified after she graduated from high school, she decided she had to skate for more than just herself; otherwise she felt trying to make the Olympic team would be too overwhelming to even attempt. She mentions that many times during her childhood she "accepted" Jesus Christ as her Savior because she wasn't sure she had "done it right."

> Even as an adult, I wondered if my commitment was enough. I mean, I talked about my faith in presentations I made and shared my faith, but I was never really sure until 1984 when I was baptized and publicly confessed Jesus Christ as my Savior and Lord. I felt like then I didn't have to worry anymore about my salvation and I wasn't so uptight about whether or not my commitment was enough. On Judgment Day, only what's done for Christ will last.
>
> If I was going to continue skating I would use it for opportunities to share my faith. That, as well as winning medals, became my goal. I was very competitive and I loved to win, but I wanted and needed a more lasting reason to skate.

While she attended Wheaton, the school's evangelistic ministry philosophy, along with talking to other students and seeing them share their faith, persuaded her to actively share her faith. "When I saw what other students at Wheaton College were involved in," she says, "it encouraged me to speak out."

Some college athletes joke about squeezing four years of coursework into five, but Nancy (who took time off to compete) squeezed her speech and communications degree into seven. Three different presidents—Ford, Carter, and Reagan—came into office during that time. She met football player Jeff Peltz while a senior in 1980 and they got married in May of 1985.

It's no wonder she'd marry an athlete, since her family was so athletic.

As a child, Nancy shadowed her older brothers John and Mike on the ice, wearing their hand-me-down black speed skates. She could skate faster with the speed skates, she says, so she got to play with the boys, but the girls made fun of her.

> I just got their skates and played pom pom with the boys and chased them. Pom pom is a tag game played on the ice with one player in the middle who calls, "Pom pom!" starting the players' attempt at crossing the ice without being touched. Tagged players have to stay in the middle.
> All the other girls would look at my skates and make fun of them and laugh. But I loved playing with the boys. I loved being different at that point. Even though I had a lot of peer pressure from the girls and felt ostracized by them, I felt accepted by the guys. I think that feeling of being more accepted by the guys than the girls has kind of run through the rest of my life.

"But then, I just enjoyed being able to go fast. I didn't know that speed skating was an Olympic sport," she adds. Her parents took her to some area speed-skating races, and her first disappointing impression was that it was just local stuff.

As she grew up, her mother helped her understand that she could be an athlete and still be a young woman. When junior high classmates who were used to flirting with the guys would snicker in the girls' restroom because Nancy didn't wear makeup or nylons, her mother helped her put it in perspective and reassured her about her priorities.

Nancy's time was well-spent training with the boys instead of calling them on the phone. "But being ridiculed can really hurt your self-confidence," she says. "I didn't really have a group to feel a part of; I wasn't part of the 'in' group, but I wasn't part of the 'out' group either. Still, because I was successful in sports, I felt that most people looked up to me and respected me."

Later she would be criticized by female skaters who were critical of her "excessive" competitive drive.

> They criticized me for being a Christian who wanted to win and told me I shouldn't be so concerned with winning.
> They didn't understand that my goal was just to do my best—that the harder you work the harder it is to lose. Maybe they thought that a Christian shouldn't give a rip whether they won or not.
> My competitiveness came from training so hard and sacrificing so much. I depended on my parents and brothers so much for coaching and encouragement and for finances and to drive me places, that I

didn't want to disappoint them. In Olympic sports, winning and losing is so significant because you sacrifice so much. The highs are extremely high when you win and the lows are extremely low when you lose because of that. The results are so final; you can't go back and change things.

Even in school I wanted to do well on tests. I wanted to be like my brother Mike because he was a good student and my brother John, who was so versatile and good at so many things. I was upset if I didn't do well, so I'd stay up until 1:00 in the morning studying to be prepared. I put pressure on myself from within to do well.

Really, though, I just wanted to live up to my potential, which is why I trained so hard. I didn't want to just talk about my faith and not live it. I think it brings honor and glory to God when you give 100 percent. When you fulfill your ability by doing that, you can feel good about it.

Now Nancy's teaching others that same technique and drive that propelled her to success on the ice. She's coached the Junior World Team for the U.S. International Speed-skating Association, including working with two 1988 Olympic speed skaters: Mark Greenwald and David Cruikshank. Now, with a newborn it's harder, she says, but she continues coaching the Park Ridge Club and Cruikshank.

Throughout a casual conversation those coaching instincts come out. Nancy summarizes her coaching philosophy.

People started realizing that your body needs a time to rest, a time to taper off—train hard, train easy—to maximize a person's competitive fitness. My rule of thumb is always to take one rest day a week. There is no way you can *not* take one day off a week and be the best you can be. You need to replenish your carbohydrates and your mind. You need to keep loving it and being excited and "psyched." I think you *can* work day after day for a period of time, but it's going to kill you sooner or later. Coaching is not only giving the right programs but making it fun and inspiring and motivating that person to use their body to the maximum.

While her many accomplishments are satisfying, somehow when talking to Nancy, you sense that those old competitive desires might be rekindled. For her, the memories of the Olympic flame are more strongly etched in her mind than the memories of her screaming thigh muscles in training. "If I were to get back to competitive weight and if I did well at some triathlons next summer and if the kids could travel with me and if I could work out and if I could find a sponsor—I'd entertain the thought.

"I believe when you train so hard and get to the top level in your sport that you can work back up to that again. Yet I love being at home and being Mom," she says. "I don't know whether it's societal pressures making me ask myself, 'Is there more?' I may never have a full-time career—I don't want to push it and get too many irons in the fire. I want to do all things well and I need time to do that.

"Or maybe I'm feeling that as a Christian there's more work to do. I'm just a little restless, like I've got more to give in this world. I'm praying every day that I'll know. I just feel there's something else the Lord wants me to do." For now, Nancy is coaching Cruikshank, who has a great chance of qualifying for the 1992 Olympics in Albertville, France. And she and Jeff are considering having a third child. Plus there are those who feel that maybe, just maybe, she might again qualify as an Olympic speed skater.

# 13 ***Kay Yow***

## Working on the
## net results

WHILE STARTLING ALLEGATIONS about the North Carolina State men's basketball program abound in Peter Golenbock's controversial book *Personal Fouls*, there is another Wolfpack basketball squad which should be making front-page news for what it's doing *right*.

That's the Wolfpack Women, directed by 1988 Olympic coach Kay Yow. Her consistent leadership has permeated the entire distaff program.

They may be lesser known than the men's squad, but that's better than being known for lesser things.

According to the Poole Commission Report which scrutinized the men's program, fewer than 24 percent of the male basketball players since 1980 have graduated from North Carolina State. Indeed, of the forty-three players recruited during Jim Valvano's tenure, twenty-nine have been on academic warning. In 1983, the year the men's team won the national title, the team's cumulative grade point average was 1.67, with one player having a semester GPA of 0.23.[1]

The male cagers' off-court woes are well-documented, but they're still scoring big on the floor with their titles and on the fashion scene with their name-brand sportswear deals. Yet the women's team can be satisfied, knowing that commitment to integrity, fairness, and honesty bring success in the long run. The women may not have the notoriety, but they're winning by degrees—Bachelor of Arts and Bachelor of Science degrees. The

---

1. *Los Angeles Times*, (31 August 1989); Pt. III, p. 7.

influence comes straight from the top. Coach Yow emphasizes her players' scoring big in the classroom, too.

She requires all players below a certain grade-point average and all freshmen to attend a supervised nightly study hall. Attendance is nonnegotiable, but some players still object to the additional intrusion on personal time outside of daily practice. "There are some people who definitely do not want to attend that study hall because it interferes with their social life and certain freedoms and privileges," says the 5-foot-7-inch, former high school English teacher. "They feel their playing time should be earned by what they do on the court as an athlete and not by what they do in the classroom. And sometimes we have discussions about why they have to go.

"But after they've graduated, former players come back and say to me, 'Coach Yow, don't ever get rid of study hall. I didn't like it when I was here and I didn't want it, but now I know how much I needed it.'"

Kay stresses players' learning their textbooks as well as their playbooks and basketball manuals. Her years of coaching experience have proven that personal discipline off the court is as important as their skills on the floor. She comments:

> As a head coach, you have a certain amount of authority, but the way you use it or flaunt it is something else. You have to help the players understand that your intentions are good and that the discipline—like mandatory study hall and penalties for breaking rules—is in their best interests; that it's the behavior the coaches are concerned with and that the disciplinary measures are not against them personally. There's a saying that people don't care how much you know until they know how much you care. I've tried to coach and live by that.

Kay's personal discipline standards were influenced by her parents, Hilton and Libby Yow, while growing up in rural Gibsonville, North Carolina, population 5,000. Although she was selected Most Valuable Player and an all-conference basketball player four times, Kay's high school highlight was making the All-State squad and playing in the North Carolina East-West All-Star game. She credits her parents, who celebrated their fiftieth wedding anniversary in August 1989, with teaching her about commitment and personal discipline.

> I knew my parents were in total control because they reinforced what they said. I was always reassured that discipline wasn't something

that was done *against* me, but was done *for* me. They disciplined with love, and that's the key to the whole matter of authority. Even though as a kid I didn't understand it, my parents would say, "This hurts me worse than it will hurt you—for you to not be able to go to this event tonight or to ground you hurts me worse than it will hurt you." It would make me even more mad because they said it.

Then later, you understand the discipline perfectly. It's hard to discipline when you care so much about people, yet you know in order for your players to become the people they need to become, it takes discipline.

Kay has continually impressed those same childhood lessons on those whom she influences.

Moreover, she says,

All of that is important to communicate so that the discipline is a healthy, positive experience and so they can grow as a person. It comes when you establish guidelines and treat all people equally. It's very important that your best player, your star, wouldn't be exempt from these expectations—that across the board you'll enforce the rules in a fair way; that you have already put forth your expectations of behavior and if they're not met, then the discipline and penalty have already been set. And it doesn't waver as to who it is. The discipline is for the behavior and not against the person.

She requires punctuality for team meetings, practice, and appointments with trainers and coaches. "When people aren't, you have to take disciplinary measures," she says, gently but firmly disallowing most excuses. "As a coach, you have to stand firm to the guidelines you have set, for there's no strength to them if they're not enforced. The Bible, especially Proverbs, has been an encouragement for me to try to be strong in that area; to have high expectations and demands and then to follow up on those."

Kay, the eldest of four children, was born March 14, 1942. She later was joined by brother Ronnie, who was followed by sisters Debbie and Susan. Coaching interests run in the family: Susan, a 1976 Kodak all-American for Kay at NCS, was her 1988 Olympic team assistant and is currently head coach at Drake University in Des Moines, Iowa. Debbie, now married to Dr. William Bowden, raises funds for the University of North Carolina in Greensboro and is associate athletic director, after first having coached basketball at the University of Kentucky, Oral Roberts University, and the University of Florida. Ronnie is a house-painting contractor in Greensboro.

Kay's parents, Hilton and Libby, had grown up together and been married in Gibsonville, and both had enjoyed playing basketball on the numerous mill teams in local industrial and recreational leagues. After they'd hung up their sneakers and retired, every so often their athletic children could cajole them into playing some ball in the backyard. Most times were fun-filled and without mishap. But when Libby was forty-eight, misfortune struck, and she broke both wrists playing basketball in a Sunday afternoon backyard pickup game. Her career as a beautician was put on hold while she recovered.

"She didn't want to play," Kay says now about that incident over twenty years ago, "But we talked her into it because we needed another player." The court was sloped toward the backboard, and Libby, in trying to catch a lead pass, slipped in the slanted area and tried to break her fall with her hands. "We felt terrible. . . . And she felt foolish. It's pretty hard to tell someone you broke both wrists playing basketball when you're forty-eight!"

Life was fun growing up in the mill town, where Kay attended Sunday morning worship regularly with her family, as well as going Sunday and Wednesday evenings, and to youth group meetings. But when she went away to college at East Carolina University, her church attendance declined. Outside of her mother's wishes, she had no reason to go.

"I didn't go at all because I had never come to know the Lord in a personal way," she says now. Playing basketball in the winter and pitching in competitive Amateur Softball Association slow-pitch leagues and tournaments in the summer filled her time. Kay was outstanding, making more than thirty softball all-tournament teams, twice tabbed Most Valuable Player of her ASA Regional, and also selected to the ASA Open Class World Tournament first team while with the Graham (North Carolina) Rubi-Otts. There was a lot in life to discover beyond the church steeple.

Kay graduated from East Carolina in 1964 with an English degree and began teaching and coaching at North Carolina high schools. Over the next five years, her teams won 77 percent of their games, along with four conference titles. Then, Kay stepped up to Elon College, where her Golden Girls were 57–19 in five years, topped by consecutive state titles in 1974 and 1975.

In those embryonic days of women's intercollegiate athletics, it was David vs. Goliath—smaller private colleges competed against big state universities in postseason play—and frequently the smaller schools won. The Association of Intercollegiate Athletics for Women governed women's intercollegiate competition prior to being absorbed into the previously male-dominated National Collegiate Athletic Association.

Actually, smaller schools like Elon had the advantage in those days. Larger universities were often dominated by a football mentality and women's competitions were club sports at best with no financing or budgets from the universities they represented. But women sought equal access to the playing fields, and universities responded by offering increased scholarships and budgets.

North Carolina State was one of those, and in 1975 recruited Kay to start the school's program as the first full-time paid women's basketball coach and coordinator of women's athletics.

The job came equipped with an office and an accessibility unknown in the bureaucratic structure of today's athletic programs. Fans could walk right in and sit down and speak to the coach. And the coaches were thankful for the interest. One of those interested in Kay's program was Laurie, a representative of a campus Christian group. After walking in and introducing herself, she began meeting weekly with Kay. She requested a team meeting where she and friends could share the claims of Christ with the ballplayers. At first Kay welcomed Laurie's interest, but the second, third, and subsequent visits bordered on tedium. She says, "Laurie spoke openly about Christ and God, and at a tempo I was not used to. Sometimes I dreaded seeing her come."

Kay's discomfort was not apparent to Laurie; it was masked carefully by her previous church background. "When she would talk about the meeting, on the outside I was all favorable, but on the inside, I couldn't really see requiring my players to come. I was concerned about what they might think of me, and I was into caring a whole lot about what other people thought."

Finally Laurie's persistence paid off, and Kay hurriedly scheduled a team meeting; so hurriedly in fact, that Kay didn't have time to consult her team captains who usually would be brought in on such a decision.

Laurie kept coming by and asking to meet with the team. She really got to me. It finally became easier to have the meeting and to get it over with. Maybe then we would have something more to talk about than planning for it and more reason to get together every week.

I called the meeting and told Laurie and her friends that they could meet with the team for a *short*—specifically short—meeting. After Laurie and her friends were finished, they passed out some cards on which you were to indicate whether you wanted more information, to meet again, or perhaps if you had prayed the prayer of salvation.

The meeting was at 6:30 after practice, and at 8:00 Laurie called me and was all excited that one person had prayed that prayer.

That person was me.

The Lord had impressed Kay through all those earlier meetings that she needed to know Him in a personal way, and she had responded.

"When I finally made the decision to have that meeting, then I was personally ready. Where no one else had accepted the Lord—although some wanted more information—I prayed that prayer of salvation."

Kay eagerly embraced her newly found faith. "I had read the Bible plenty, but it had very little meaning until the Holy Spirit brought meaning to it and until the Holy Spirit became part of my life and revealed it to me. It's hard to believe you could be in church that long and never understand the message."

Throughout her coaching experience, Kay has learned to share her beliefs about God with her team members through the person that she is. "It's all because of my personal relationship with the Lord. My discipline is love-based. My motivation is love-based. It's because of who He is that I do what I do.

"And I continue to grow in Him more and more every day. I believe every year I do things better because of my growth in Him, because I try to do things as He would have me to do them. Because I have a long way to go, right?" But Kay also is ready to verbally profess what God means to her.

Certainly the Lord gives me opportunities to share one-on-one. When He provides the opportunity and it's there, then I share. My faith is not something that I ever try to force on people, but I'm willing to share when God presents the time and the people, and He brings them to me. Then they are ready and I'm ready.

We never want others to see Christianity as a personal putdown, as if we don't smoke or do this or that because we think we're better than anyone else. We want them to see that our relationship with Christ is vital, that it's exciting and alive, and that we depend on it.

There's nothing like a vibrant, strong personal relationship with the Lord. It's not about right and wrong. Right and wrong will come about because of your relationship with the Lord. The Lord Himself will get you on the right track. Righteousness is His, not ours. And we don't want others to see our personal righteousness, but His.

Kay is careful about too hurriedly trying to influence those around her, including coaching peers and athletes, preferring to wait for the Lord to bring opportunities. On the other hand, she has a boldness about her faith that even gives her the courage to risk arrest or possible dismissal from coaching national teams.

In a highly publicized incident prior to the Goodwill Games and World Championships in Moscow the summer of 1986, Kay was questioned by Soviet authorities for attempting to conceal Bibles in her personal luggage. The American media overreacted, and Kay was labeled a religious fanatic. She was threatened with losing her international coaching status by the Amateur Basketball Association of the United States (ABAUSA, basketball's governing body). But for Kay, her faith cannot be separated from her actions. Nearly three years later, she says,

> I want to be able to take Bibles wherever the Lord would have me. You don't do "this" for yourself and "that" for God. It's just not something you can separate out.
>
> I felt a need to do what the Lord would have me to do. It was not a big thing to me. My concern has always been for the people who might not have a Bible to read.
>
> See, I just never even thought of it as courage. I never even thought of it as being offensive to the Soviets until I got back and saw the way the newspaper article was written. I never even saw the other side until then. I felt it was an easy thing to do because the Lord made it an easy thing to do.

Despite that controversy, Kay's coaching reputation is highly respected in basketball circles. Kay has coached U.S. national teams since 1979, and has a remarkable 21–1 head coaching record in international competition. Kay's 1981 World University Games squad finished 4–1 to win the silver medal. In the summer of 1986, the U.S. women twice defeated the Soviets—the first time in twenty-nine years that the Americans had beaten the Soviet women and, remarkably, it was in Moscow. The women cagers were led by Cheryl Miller, Teresa Edwards, and Anne Donovan. They took gold medals in the Goodwill Games, then later won the World Championships.

Returning with those inspirational wins, Kay, the 1984 Olympic assistant coach (to the University of Tennessee's Pat

Head Summitt) was named as the 1988 Olympic coach. There was another successful season at N.C. State (24–7) for the coach who has averaged over twenty wins a season. Then it was time to begin earnest preparations for the XXIII Olympiad in Seoul.

Kay, always the realist, had never really dreamed about playing basketball in the Olympics, and it wasn't until the 1980s that she thought coaching a team might be a possibility. Women's basketball initially was contested on the 1976 Olympic program in Montreal. In 1980, the U.S. boycotted the Summer Olympics. So in 1984, when Kay was named assistant Olympic coach, it was only the second time American women had entered Olympic basketball competition.

"I was always excited about the Olympics, but never had the opportunity as a player," she recalls. "I could play in the back yard by myself and pretend I was making the final shot of a tournament, or to win the conference, but to pretend to be in the Olympics was never really a serious dream because it was never a possibility."

While Kay was gearing up preparations, just a year prior to the Seoul Games, in a routine check-up doctors discovered cancerous lumps in her breast tissue. During August of 1987, a modified radical mastectomy was performed, and twenty lymph nodes in her right breast were removed. While she had piled up plenty of statistics on the basketball court, she had never wanted to *become* one in this kind of arena. Statistics show that one in ten women will have breast cancer. The Russians were nothing compared to this opponent. This battle was for life or death. There were two agonizing weeks between discovery of the cancer and the exploratory surgery.

> It was a great shock—unbelievable. I couldn't take in what was happening to me. But the Lord showed me not to panic and to accept what I couldn't change and not wallow in self-pity. He can take anything in life and turn it to good. I know.
>
> He says when we're weak, He's strong. He caused me to totally depend on Him—even today, because cancer is not a disease you can totally beat for good. You can win a battle, but you don't know when it might reoccur. And having had the surgery, the scars remind me of my great dependence on Him. I need to depend on Him whether I have cancer or not.

She quietly adds that it was not all bad to be reminded of one's dependence on God. "It helps keep your perspective and balance. It's good to learn to depend on God."

Though weakened, within two months, Kay was back on the basketball court coaching and counting her blessings that her health was being restored. And yet there was another personal trial, with her mother Libby being diagnosed with another threatening form of breast cancer called hairy-cell lymphoma. While still battling her own health problems, Kay was further concerned by her mother's illness.

With all the additional stress, perhaps Kay would be unable to perform her coaching duties. At the time of her surgery, the Olympic team tryouts were a little more than six months away. And while Kay was recovering, there was some doubt expressed about her ability to coach the U.S. women's Olympic basketball team. Because of Kay's steady faith in God, the doubt turned out to be unfounded. She explains:

> I didn't have a fear about not being able to coach, because the Lord was dealing with me. But there was a concern that entered other people's minds that perhaps something would happen and I wouldn't be able to handle those duties. But it was in God's hands. He knew better than I did. He knows the total plan.
>
> We're to work on trusting Him. It was a real time for my personal growth and digging deeper and more complex roots into God's Word. God is sovereign over all that happens. He is totally in control. It was my part to do all I could to recover, and if things went well, I would recover.

In addition to Kay's own health concerns and those of her mother that winter of 1987–88, there was adversity in the form of player injuries which depleted her Wolfpack squad (which was 24–7 in 1986–87 and had earned North Carolina State its third Atlantic Coast Conference Tournament championship in ten years) of seven scholarship players. Kay was forced to recruit soccer players to fill in. The 10–17 final season record in 1987–88 was Kay's first losing season at North Carolina State.

That was disappointing, but shortly thereafter, in April, the Olympic tryouts opened. They say bad news travels in bunches, but this was more like an invading army was camped on her doorstep. Kay discovered knee injuries would disable two of her top candidates: four-time all-American Cheryl Miller and University of Texas standout Clarissa Davis (who would later gain recognition as the 1988 female collegiate basketball Player of the Year, opposite Arizona's Sean Elliott, the male Player of the Year). Once again, Kay's faith and trust in God would be tested.

"Injuries are always a cause for great concern, but it's also something out of my control," she offers realistically. "I try not to worry about things I have no control over. I try to concentrate on things I have control over."

She definitely had control over her basketball team, and in Seoul, the American women beat Czechoslovakia 87–81, Yugoslavia 101–74, and China 94–79 in pool play to enter the gold-medal round. There they faced the Soviet Union in the semi-finals, defeating them 102–88 before again meeting Yugoslavia for the gold medal. Winning 77–70, the women had successfully defended the gold medal they won in the Los Angeles Games.

"To beat the Soviet Union [Kay's third win in three tries] was a thrill only next to winning the gold medal. Having beaten Yugoslavia in pool play, it was even harder the second time. The only thing tougher than winning is winning again," she says, praising her Olympic staff. "The two assistant coaches, the trainers, the manager, and the assistant executive director for the ABAUSA were incredible—a fantastic staff that couldn't be better.

"And the players themselves—I couldn't have had better cooperation from the players. What a fantastic team to work with! Their willingness to put the team first and themselves second is why we won. They maintained positive attitudes even when there were injuries or a lack of playing time."

Kay cites particularly co-captain and two-time Olympian Anne Donovan, who lost her starting position, yet ignited the team in the gold-medal game.

> She came in and gave us the boost we needed, and maintained such a positive attitude throughout her whole experience. She didn't get as much playing time in some games as she would have liked, but she encouraged other people.
>
> And others didn't get to play the positions they wanted, but had to take positions that were in the best interests of the team. Yet they came through and played to the best of their abilities. That's what we want and that's why we won. They had the talent, but they never could have won the gold medal unless they were the *people* that they were.

Kay continues, with a coaching dictum she often uses. "They were able to rise above the circumstance and have attitude control over circumstance control. Circumstances too often control one's attitude. If we had let circumstances have control, we wouldn't have the gold medal today, because there were many adverse circumstances." And she relates the Olympic effort to Jesus' example in the New Testament.

> Because of the things the Lord had to face, He had to have attitude control. He wouldn't let circumstances control Him. In Philippians 2 it says that we should have the attitude which He had, and it explains in detail what that attitude was—putting others ahead of ourselves, not being selfish or ambitious. That attitude applies in sports and every other situation. Your attitude is so important in being successful. Attitude is the key to success.

Following her Olympic accomplishments, Kay returned to North Carolina State, and the team rebounded to a 24–7 record, ranked thirteenth nationally, and made the NCAA playoffs for the seventh time in eight years. She also was named honorary fundraising chairwoman for the Lineberger Cancer Research Institute at the University of North Carolina. The goal of one million dollars would be successfully met by the time her chairmanship ended in December of 1989.

All told, Kay says that living successfully in overcoming adversity beats "becoming successful."

> By living successfully, you don't have to worry about *becoming* successful because you already are. We have the ability to overcome obstacles and adversity. We have to make commitments to people and to biblical principles like honesty, integrity, loyalty, and fairness. We have to consecrate our lives to Jesus and have Him at the center of our lives. And finally we have to be able to cope with prosperity and achievement. If you're going to conquer your problems, you're going to have to do those things to be successful.

Kay's success at the Olympic Games, the World Championships, the Goodwill Games, the Pan American Games, and the World University Games has gained her great prominence in the coaching profession. Yet her faith, not success, remains the driving force in her life.

She quotes from Mark 8:36 (NKJV), "What will it profit a man if he gains the whole world, and loses his own soul?" and Matthew 6:33 (NKJV), "Seek first the kingdom of God and His righteousness," as foundations to her faith. She explains, paraphrasing a favorite hymn. "I'd rather have Jesus than silver or gold [medals and trophies], I'd rather have Jesus than championships or riches untold," she says.

God provides basketball and sports and it's a very important part of my life, but my faith, my family, and my friends come before basketball.

They say cancer changes you and you see things differently and do things differently. Values do change when you're facing death. You just don't know what the outcome will be with cancer. You have to face it and think what really matters about life. Cancer provided the insight I never really gained any other way. I can't get the feeling of anxiety inside me that I had in that moment when I didn't know how extensive or what kind of cancer it was or anything about it. But I did know the Lord, and that trial just brought Him into sharper focus. It reinforced my relationship and dependence on Him.

Kay speaks frequently before civic groups, corporations, church groups, and young people's groups about those experiences. After her team won the Olympic gold medal, the demands on Kay increased dramatically, including increased correspondence from adults and young players alike. Kay conscientiously responds to these letters, noting "I want to share the Olympic dream with everybody."

She shares a story from a sermon that describes her own experiences with adversity. The pastor told about a man with a very expensive sailboat who, along with his wife, was caught in a violent storm on the open seas.

At first he prayed that the storm wouldn't destroy the boat. He'd lose all his investment. But the storm got worse. Then he prayed that the couple's lives would be spared. And yet the storm got worse. And then he prayed for his wife's life to be spared.

When we're first faced with adversity our prayers start off pretty shallow. As we come face to face with the difficulty we grow. Our prayers change and we see the adversity on a much deeper level. We see what really becomes important. The adversity helps us separate the urgent from the important.

We can identify with the man in the boat and how his prayers moved to a deeper level. Too often we pray for circumstances to change. God is free to deal with us when we're willing to trust Him for those circumstances.

Recent health checkups have been positive. Kay is also encouraged about the potential in this year's Wolfpack squad. Nearly overshadowed by all the other drama of 1988, was Kay's induction into the Women's Sports Hall of Fame where she joined Jackie Joyner-Kersee, Althea Gibson, and Wilma Rudolph, among others. The National Organization of Women voted her as the Woman of the Year in Sport. And Kay received the 1988 Carol Eckmann Award, selected by members of the Women's Basketball Coaches Association and presented to an active coach who best demonstrates sportsmanship, honesty, courage, ethical behavior, dedication to purpose, and a commitment to the student athlete. There could have been no better honoree than Kay Yow.

# Rachel McLish

## 14

## Muscling her way to the top

TWICE SHE WON the coveted Ms. Olympia bodybuilding championship.

Once she won the world title.

In her sport's first few years she dominated all competitions.

Yet, while still at her peak, she retired in protest over the direction of women's bodybuilding, calling it perverted and masculinizing. Being in good shape is one thing, she says; using steroids to achieve that is another.

Those crashing and clanging silvery metal weights have brought her much material success: an expensive desert home featuring a marble entryway and rooms tastefully accented by bronze sculptures, Oriental pieces, modern art, and classic oil paintings. Outside is a beautifully landscaped pool, a spa, and a championship tennis court. In the back is a guest house that may someday serve as an office and home gym. Though she says she now prefers the more relaxed Palm Springs lifestyle, the bright lights have once again drawn her toward Los Angeles.

Rachel McLish, star of an October 1989, hour-long CBS television special called "Woman of the Twenty-first Century," is making the transition from bodybuilding superstar to aspiring actress. In the show, she explored how women can pursue a healthy and physically fit lifestyle, covering topics such as self-defense, weight training and aerobics, dance for exercise and enjoyment, burnout in elite women athletes, and sports and family recreation time.

With fiancé, Hollywood film producer/adviser Ron Samuels close by, there's great potential. He previously has guided the careers of actresses Lindsey Wagner and Jaclyn Smith, among others.

Rachel's sweaty ordeal has become a sweet deal. Already, she has contracted with one of the nation's largest discount retailers to endorse her own signature line of workout wear. Those iron plates stacked in the weight room like forsaken flapjacks seem to have piled up like Fort Knox gold. She moves in social circles unknown to most bodybuilders.

For instance, Rachel caught the bouquet when retired tennis star Chris Evert married Andy Mill. She happily shares a snapshot of herself at the wedding, smiling and hugging Chris.

A stunning photo of Rachel appears in singer/songwriter Kenny Rogers's assortment of celebrity portraits, *Your Friends and Mine*. From stars like George Burns, Elizabeth Taylor, and Dolly Parton to three of the four living former presidents of the United States, the country singer photographed seventy-seven famous people for his collector's coffee-table book. Even among so many interesting portraits, Rachel's captivating black and white photo really lifts eyebrows. She seems to have had that effect on a lot of people in the last decade.

Now living in Southern California, with homes in Los Angeles and Rancho Mirage, it's a long way physically and figuratively from her Hispanic roots in Harlingen, Texas, at the southernmost tip of the central United States. Even though her near-cult status in competitive bodybuilding would seem to prevent it, Rachel professes a desire to retain her small-town freshness.

She says she enjoys living in the desert and not having the hassles of L.A. That's not to say she's resting easy playing tennis with the country club ladies. She's busy promoting her energetic lifestyle, the health and fitness business, and working out. Her kitchen table holds her two most important communication links for doing so. One takes her outward and the other one takes her upward: her telephone and her leather-bound Bible. Both seem well used. But it's the Bible and her personal relationship with Jesus Christ that Rachel credits as the source of her success, giving her an inner strength that has allowed her to push through some incredible pain barriers in and out of the weight room.

Although Rachel has written two books, the best-selling *Flex Appeal* (in its ninth printing) and, more recently, *Perfect Parts: A World Champion's Guide to "Spot" Slimming, Shaping and Strengthening Your Body* (over a hundred thousand in sales by its fourth printing), it was a 1984 movie appearance that muscled her out of competition and into the marketplace.

That docudrama, titled *Pumping Iron II: The Women,* portrayed a fictional Las Vegas contest called the Caesar's World Cup. Movie makers promised Rachel, the then reigning world titlist, that the movie would do for her career what *Pumping Iron* reputedly did in launching Arnold Schwarzenegger's marquee value beyond sweaty weight rooms. The contestants used their real names and played themselves, but the storyline was made up.

Indeed, the movie did launch Rachel's career, but in totally unanticipated ways.

The changing emphases in women's bodybuilding was so unacceptable to Rachel that, as quietly as possible for a reigning champion, she exited the world of competitive bodybuilding altogether. In protest over the sport's direction, she even quit reading the bodybuilding trade magazines in which she frequently had been featured.

Within two years she had signed on as a spokesperson for a large national chain of health and fitness centers instead.

When she spoke out for femininity and against steroids and masculinity in bodybuilding, Rachel was ridiculed, especially by feminists, she says. That group had previously embraced her because her musculature and strength and willingness to reach new limits seemed to promote their women's-rights platform. But when the movie portrayed her as both feminine and religious, feminists scoffed. The final edits, over which Rachel had no control, trivialized her faith in God and depicted the tanning booth as more important to her than the weight room. Rachel remains adamant that she participated in the movie in order to force discussion of the steroid issue.

Life had been much simpler growing up in cozy Harlingen (population 40,000) as the fourth of five children (four girls and a boy) in the Elizondo family. "I guess I had an average childhood," she offers. With a close family and neighborhood kids that all grew up together and attended the same schools, Rachel felt secure. "I thought I had everything—until you travel, you know, that's all relative. But even in retrospect, I think Harlingen (in the Rio Grande Valley) was a very fine place to grow up," she says.

My dad was aware of being physically fit. My first association with weights was through him. I can remember his barbells, dumbbells, and weight bench from when I was four or five years old. I just thought it was the neatest thing that my dad was so strong. So I always associated muscles and strength with my dad, which was positive. And it wasn't anything new to me when I started lifting weights. I just thought it was a good way to stay in shape.

With no "girls' sports" available in South Texas in the midseventies, Rachel turned to ballet lessons along with cheerleading and the dance squad as acceptable alternatives. Her observation that "all the school athletic money went to the guys, the football team and all that—just the usual story back then" typifies the feelings of many would-be female athletes of that era. "When I was in high school they might have started girls' track meets or something like that."

After graduating from high school, she attended Pan American University thirty miles down the road in Edinburg. When the dorm food and inactivity made her feel like a desk potato, she discovered a health club and says, "I totally fell in love with the atmosphere. I had never seen a health club before, and I thought it was terrific."

Attracted by the upscale carpeted weight rooms, mirrored walls, tasteful decor, and of course, the gleaming iron weights and racks—and lacking money for a membership—Rachel applied for a job at the club. It eventually financed her education. Pursuing a college degree in health and physical education with a minor in nutrition, Rachel put her anatomy and physiology knowledge to work at the club, trying innovative methods and devising more effective workouts as well as reducing diets. Receiving positive responses from thousands of members was very gratifying.

"I thought, 'This is what I want to do with my life!'" she says.

Rachel tirelessly promoted the health club, recruiting new members and guiding the regular afficionados.

The club's success led to a second club opening in Brownsville, twenty-six miles away, and an opportunity for Rachel to form a partnership with the owner to seek investors for an improved facility.

"I became a gym owner when I was twenty. It was just fabulous and I loved it," says Rachel, who directed the women's activities for a club that had one thousand members by the time it opened its doors. "It was very, very exciting and I just loved it.

"I wasn't shy. I'd go to Rotary Clubs, Lion Clubs, even sororities, and give speeches on how our club could help them with their fitness," she says. "It's a service-oriented business, and I personally had counseled every woman who came in. We talked about their goals, and we would check their cards and measurements every week. I'd give them lots of personal attention and encourage them and show them I cared."

She says the women loved working with weights because they got results, but she had to be careful with her terminology. In a *Wall Street Journal* article, Rachel remarked that "South Texas is not exactly a trend-setting kind of place. The macho man doesn't want his woman to be building muscles. Of course, he'd like her to get her bottom a little tighter or to firm up her thighs. So I'd use words like *firm* and *tone* and *tighten* instead of *bodybuilding*, but it's the same thing. It's all in the way you present it."[1]

She encouraged the women to use weights because she knew that lifting was the quickest way of getting in shape. But from her background in physiology and physical education, she also knew that it took aerobic exercise to burn more calories. "So we combined aerobics and bodybuilding with a low-fat diet—all the things people are doing now—but we started doing it in South Texas a long time ago."[2]

In promoting the Brownsville club's 1980 opening, Rachel began training for the first-ever women's international bodybuilding competition, an event headlined by Lisa Lyon (the first unofficial women's bodybuilding champion) and publicized in the bodybuilding magazines. Years of counseling thousands of women in her area gave Rachel insights as to what would work best for her.

Rachel, impressed by the feminine and articulate Lyon, with whom she agreed philosophically about building strength in a woman's body and who was her first role model, prepared for the Atlantic City contest by intensifying her training: running eight miles, then isolating every body part—the pecs, abdominals, glutes and delts, biceps, triceps, quadriceps, and every ceps she could find—and polishing her posing routine.

"All those women in Atlantic City were flexing their muscles and calling themselves bodybuilders, and I remember thinking then, 'Hey, wait a minute. This is what we've been doing in South Texas for the past five years. This isn't anything new.'

"So I went up there to promote the health clubs and really hype it up and ended up getting into the competition on television."

Rachel's physique won her a smashing victory. Clippings told her story worldwide. Pretty heady stuff for a small-town Texas girl.

---

1. *Wall Street Journal* (19 January 1988).
2. Ibid.

Indeed, she felt that everything had fit together, from her father's example during her childhood to studying health and physical education to working at the club.

"I had the background. I had paid the dues. I knew the answer to most questions about fitness, about muscles and everything," she says. "Performing came very naturally to me after being on stage with ballet and being in front of crowds as a cheerleader. What we'd built through our clubs in South Texas, competitive bodybuilding enabled me to continue on a worldwide level."

Along with the title came appearance requests from all over the world. The post office would forward letters addressed simply Rachel McLish, Harlingen, Texas. "I was swamped with offers from all over the world and even though I wanted to take it slower and carefully consider things, I also didn't want to waste the opportunities," Rachel says. Her first jaunt included stops in Japan, Sweden, Norway, Finland, and Germany.

Soon, competitive bodybuilding opportunities forced her to choose between traveling or staying with her hometown health club, which had grown tremendously under her expertise. "I started getting lots of money for just showing up and talking about fitness and body building; this new thing that women were doing."

While at Pan American University, Rachel had met and married a local baseball star named John McLish. John, son of former major leaguer Calvin McLish (who was also a pitching coach in Montreal and Milwaukee) had been drafted out of high school but had wanted to go to college before signing pro. But by the age of twenty-two, John found himself out of baseball and instead singing country ballads in dinner theaters. Rachel and John were married for only a year and a half before the marriage dissolved. While there were glamorous opportunities for Rachel in bodybuilding, John had offers from record companies but was content to stay in South Texas.

"At that point our marriage had deteriorated, and we weren't mature enough to go to counseling and really know how to make it work. Because of the hurts, we didn't want to work through it at the time—I didn't want to work through it at the time," she corrects herself. "My priorities were just a little mixed up. But who knows if it would have been different?

"The marriage was a failure. We had gone through premarriage counseling classes at our church and they taught us about income taxes, about how to buy a house, and about budgeting our money. I wish they would have said, 'This is what marriage is about: two

people becoming one person in Christ.' That's the most important principle. Even when we were married it was like we were in
college, only living together. It was like now that we were married, sex was legal."

She's candidly remorseful about the failed marriage, but it did
have one everlasting life-changing aspect: When John vowed to
read through the entire Bible in one year, Rachel determined
to find out what that meant.

> I knew something was lacking in my life. I would go to everything my
> church had to offer, and it wasn't really satisfying me.
>
> So once I started reading the New Testament, I began understand-
> ing about Jesus being the Lamb and the significance of the Cross and
> how He shed His blood for me. And I began to understand what the
> priests were saying because I was coming into a personal relationship
> with Jesus Christ. You can repeat those same prayers a million times
> in a lifetime and not know what you're saying because you're just
> blindly mimicking.
>
> As a child growing up I always wanted a Bible to be able to read for
> myself, but I never got one. We'd have to repeat those things after
> the priest over and over, and it was pretty meaningless to me. After I
> went to college I didn't go to church for about four years except for
> Christmas and stuff like that with my family.

Finally, Rachel purchased her own Bible so that she, too, could
read through it.

"Reading the Bible made me understand who God was, what
He was about. Then when I went to church I could understand
the meaning, but I wondered about others there—'Does this
have meaning to them or are they just here physically like I was?'"

Rachel's spiritual quest also took her to some very different
churches. Some were too free in their worship style for her taste.
"It was too new to me and I was starting to freak out. Because I
didn't feel comfortable worshiping the way they did, it made me
feel like I wasn't saved." Her mother thought she was weird, she
says, because she was talking about God and Jesus and being saved
and the Second Coming. "She thought I was getting involved in
something like Jonestown! She didn't want me to get involved
in some kind of cult."

Rachel had been given a book by two friends. The book told
about prophecies and the Rapture. Intrigued, she called one of
them to come over and then prayed the prayer of salvation with
her. "That book scared the wits out of me and led me into

becoming a believer. It was more of a conversion based on the fear of not wanting to miss out and not one of real beliefs. I didn't understand it fully," she recalls about that time. "But fear doesn't make for a true conversion. It took me a while to grow in my faith."

Still adjusting to her divorce, Rachel started directing her newly discovered zeal for the Lord into her bodybuilding career. "When you are a new believer you're sometimes overzealous for the wrong reasons. You really need to be grounded in the Word and perhaps share your personal enthusiasm but not force the issue," she says, hinting that perhaps she may have been insensitive on occasion. "I had thought, 'Okay, God. Here I am. I am going out to save the world for You!' But during that time I really started maturing in the Word, and I realized God could only use me when I trusted Him to open the doors for sharing my faith."

After moving to the mecca of bodybuilding, Southern California, Rachel was invited to a good Bible-teaching church in Los Angeles by a friend. "Mark had noticed that I had all these little tracts and booklets. He called me and said, 'Oh by the way, in case you ever want to go to church—I know how tough it is to find a good church in a new place—and I know this really good Bible-teaching church.' Mark was my first Christian friend in California, and he really helped me a lot; he really, really did." As Rachel listened to that pastor, John MacArthur of Grace Community Church in the San Fernando Valley, explain what the Bible meant, her life and priorities gradually solidified.

After she'd won the U.S. Women's Bodybuilding title in 1980 in Atlantic City, two subsequent Ms. Olympia titles, and a 1982 World Championship, the bodybuilding movie opportunity (one of many) surfaced. Rachel insisted that it discuss steroid use among bodybuilders and was reassured it would present the important issues. Instead, as she regretfully discovered, the script's editing emphasized what Rachel felt were side issues.

The movie pits Rachel against Bev Francis, an ultramuscular Australian whose massive body was a product of power lifting. Her trainers put Bev—the world's strongest woman and the best in her sport—on a strict diet to decrease her body fat percentage, taught her some poses, and called her a bodybuilder.

Rachel terms the movie a "real, but staged competition" with legitimate judges and audience but not a recognized title competition. The women trained hard to be in top form and competed like it was a real contest, not just for a movie.

The movie dealt with the question of muscle mass in women's bodybuilding. One side said, "If women's bodybuilding is about muscularity like the men's, then Bev Francis should win because she's the most muscular. If it's not, then it's just a beauty contest." Opinion was divided at that point as to what the winning female bodybuilder should look like.

They needed me for the movie because I was the reigning titlist in women's bodybuilding, and they sold me on the idea that it would do for my career what *Pumping Iron* supposedly did for Arnold Schwarzenegger's. They promised to discuss the innermost issues of women's bodybuilding (which I thought to be steroids).

In the movie they created an issue that didn't exist—myself against Bev Francis. The most important issue, they totally ignored: the steroid issue. It's not about masculinity or femininity; the issue is using them or not using them. That's the determining factor of how masculine or how nonfeminine you will be. There were competitors definitely on steroids at the time, and not only is it unhealthy, it's very unethical.

Women's bodybuilding was a new sport but they didn't allow it to evolve naturally, with the women working within the confines of their bodies and adding muscularity naturally each year. Promoters became overanxious because of the movie, wanting to judge women's muscle mass and definition the same way they judge men's—the bigger the better.

"Femininity" is a difficult issue for female athletes and no one can fully define what it means for each individual, except in terms of physiological aspects of various hormonal levels. Yet Rachel is certain of one thing.

"I have always said there is a difference between a muscular-looking woman and a manly-looking woman. Lifting weights and working out in the field is not going to make you look like a man. Altering your hormonal makeup *is* going to do it. Muscularity isn't the issue. Drugs is the issue. No activity will ever change a woman the way steroids do. The users take the same type of drug therapy that precedes a sex-change operation. So chemically, they are men. My point was these women should be competing on stage with men.

"The movie makers avoided the real issue and not once did we hear about steroids. Every chance I'd get I would try to focus on that. Instead, they even tried to question whether or not I was using a padded bra! They ended up in the movie disqualifying nearly all my swimsuits for trivial things like metallic thread or sequins. That was the first time the promoters had ever made an issue out of posing suits.

"They just sprung it on me. I was frustrated because I kept saying the real issue was steroids. I felt used. Then I had to go out and promote the movie because of the contract I had.

"As far as my bodybuilding career, it was going great until that movie made a lie out of the competition. It was really a farce but because it was a movie I hoped no one would really believe it—or even care."

Looking for answers, Rachel again turned to the Bible for insight.

I read in the Bible that there are certain things that pertain to females and certain things that pertain to males. Bodybuilding really gave me a lesson in how God wanted females to be. I mean, there are distinct roles, and neither is more important than the other in God's eyes. But I had to deal with the feminists when *Pumping Iron II* was released because they thought I was really detrimental to the feminist movement. Even though at first they embraced me as a bodybuilder simply because I met their ideals, they then spurned me.

The feminists embraced the bodybuilders initially because of the idea that "women are limitless in their power and strength." They liked me then because I was the first champion who introduced this so-called new physical form to the world. Later they criticized me for being "too pretty, too feminine, and too limiting as to what women can do."

Who are they glorifying, anyway? I told them they were glorifying male characteristics with the direction they were taking—how can they have the nerve to call themselves feminists? If they are feminists, they should be glorifying and embracing characteristics that are female—not male.

The desire in my heart was always promoting good health through exercise, lifting weights, and utilizing good nutrition. It was always important to be all you can be as a woman. Once you give up that, you lose. You lose everything when you lose your identity and try to become something you physically cannot be. You might win a competition but lose everything you have as a woman—your identity—that's YOU!

A lot of those women I know would have identity crises in the gym because it affected their psyche so much.

Steroids, derivatives of the testosterone hormone which turns boys into men, can deepen a woman's voice, increase facial hair, and cause severe mental and emotional problems. Statistics show it causes cancer of the liver and kidneys and clogs the arteries, heightening the risk of a heart attack. The damage is irreversible.

Short-term strength and muscle mass gains are dangerously off-set by long-term side effects. "Being a champion is not winning a title with steroids. It's the character you've gained in pushing through the pain barrier and realizing what you've worked hard to build."

Rachel worked the next year preparing for what would be her final competitive bodybuilding contest, the 1984 Ms. Olympia. Inwardly she vowed to "train for the whole year to show them that I am a champion, that I am an athlete. I had been training longer than most of those women on stage and I knew what it was about. I got very muscular. I mean, I *peaked* for that one competition because at that point I knew they had decided to go with the bigger, more muscular women."

A larger than life-size black and white photo of Rachel flexing her back dominates a wall of Rachel's home. Incredible mass and muscular definition earned her only a disappointing second. Once again the ugly issue of steroids arose. Rachel questioned how the winner could put on fifteen pounds of mass in seven months. Rachel says that's an impossibility even for a male to achieve naturally.

> But I'd proven to myself that I could get into extraordinary shape. And yet I knew it was time to move on with my life because I couldn't fight this steroid issue alone. Using steroids never appealed to me. I have never even flirted with the idea, because I thought it was horrible. *And* it went against my philosophy of why you lift weights in the first place—to make your body *more* feminine, *more* attractive, *more* healthy. There's no way—win and yet destroy my body at the same time? *And* become ugly?
>
> What they were doing was just the opposite: tearing down their bodies by using drugs and steroids just for the sake of winning. What I see now in many women bodybuilders represents a perversion of the female gender. The competition and what you see on TV with the extreme muscularity, the he/she looking women and the androgenous look is really perverted.
>
> You have to be one with your Creator and have to know Him and why He created you. Lifting weights and having a healthy body is only one aspect of that. I could only be an example of what you could accomplish without steroids, but after I came in second it hurt. It was a turning point in my life. If that's what they wanted they could count me out! I severed my association with competitive women's bodybuilding, but I never really blasted the establishment because I knew from experience whatever I said would be magnified, and probably inaccurately.

Her restraint was wise. But as she searched Scripture for understanding and comfort, she says she still felt unappreciated—
like the disciples who were told to shake the dust from their
sandals when they departed a city where they were unwelcome.
"They made fun of my Christianity and would give me little digs,"
Rachel says. That hurt, but in accepting and trusting God, she
discovered the truth of that oft-quoted maxim, "When God
closes a door He opens a window." She soon secured a contract to
promote the largest health club operation in the world. "That
gave me the freedom to make other career choices."

With that, Rachel stepped out of a business in which she had
become the first superstar. She had flown the world and traveled
in style, become a celebrity, and been featured on TV and film
and in major magazines and newspapers. She'd developed a figure
men fantasize for their wives—sculpted, accented, bronzed. But
she left that lifestyle to stand up for what she believed, and retired
with her integrity intact.

Today she's still resolute about her stance against steroids. And
she feels that she's matured beyond her previous career.

"I do think bodybuilding tends to be narcissistic. The nature
of the sport dictates that all the attention be directed inward.
How do I look? And how do my muscles look?" A proper kind
of focus, though, would be no different than the intense concentration required for any creative endeavor or even operating a
computer. "When you program a computer it requires all your
attention, so bodybuilding is a job like anything else. But I realize
it can become perverted, too. I mean, you can become so en-
grossed and overconfident in yourself that you think you are
better than you really are. Like anything else, you have to put it
in its proper place."

That, to Rachel, would mean having a balance between pride
and satisfaction.

There's the pride of satisfaction and knowing you gave something
your best effort and then there's a perversion of pride. You do have to
be confident when you compete and project the image of a winner.
But off the stage, like when signing autographs, you can't have that
same attitude or it's a problem. Stardom hurts you if you don't have a
good sense of who you are. If you start believing your own publicity,
you're in trouble. Whether you're a celebrity or not, you have to have
a sense of how you are living your life and who you are with God in
order to grow and change and live positively.

I feel that's why so many stars turn to drugs as an escape. They start believing what's written. And then they realize there's nothing there in being a so-called superstar to back it up.

For myself, I handled all that attention by never believing what I read about me, because the media exaggerates everything. They'd say I was the greatest and the most beautiful and this and that—and I'm glad I didn't believe it then because later when they disagreed with me, they thought I was the worst! Ron, as a film producer, sees a lot of people who have wonderful public images; but really, they may be addicted to drugs and alcohol because they have a very low self-image. They feel they're not successful, or perhaps not successful enough.

We as human beings were not designed for glorification. The adulation that some athletes and celebrities get is impossible to handle without God's help. It's not in our nature to be deified like that. That's reserved only for God. I want to praise Him for all He's done for me. He's the One who deserves our praise.

# 15 *Jan Ripple*

## Working out,
## 9:00 to 5:00

SHE'S A WORKING MOM, sort of, she admits. She more appropriately could be called a "working-out mom."

However, that working-out mom, Jan Ripple is doing more than working 9:00 to 5:00 like movie stars Lily, Dolly, and Jane. She's working *out* from 9:00 to 5:00, or more accurately, from 6:00 to 3:00, when her children Shelly, Kyle, and Kate, arrive home from elementary school. Her extraordinary workday may typically include swimming a couple of miles, bicycling halfway to New Orleans from her Baton Rouge home, and a quick jaunt around the neighborhood. You can bet she's pounded all the pavement within a ten-mile radius of her comfortable suburban home.

Ask an average triathlete—if there is such a person—if they're working hard enough and the answer will be an unequivocal "NO!" Some spend more time training than others, but as with bookkeeping and housekeeping, there's always more to do. Various sports magazines have tabbed triathletes the "crazies" in assessing their commitment to their sport.

But not so with the 5-foot-6-inch, blonde in her midthirties. What she may feel she lacks in duration of time spent training, she more than makes up in intensity. It seems to have always been that way in Jan's athletic career, whether in competitive swimming or in simply staying in shape. Nevertheless her 1989 triathlon racing record seems to say she gets it done. Jan is recognized as one of the top five money winners in her sport and is probably second only to world champion Erin Baker of New Zealand, according to her agent, Dave McGillivray of Boston.

The former swimming champion, who qualified for the 1972 Olympic trials in the butterfly, and basketball star, who was recruited collegiately in both sports, says she has to train intelligently and plan her workouts wisely. She does so under the watchful eye of her husband Steve, a former Louisiana State University linebacker and football team captain.

Maybe she'd like to train more . . .

But there's laundry to do. Meals to cook. Grocery shopping to do. (This is one woman with whom you don't want to race grocery carts!) Dusting, baking, and sandwich making to do. And there are kids' recitals, swim meets, and soccer games. A husband to love and care for. What's a wife and mother to do?

Try a forty-five-mile bike ride for refreshment—daily.

Or swimming a couple of miles in the pool—before breakfast.

Maybe a jog around the neighborhood, too—at a nearly six-minutes-per-mile pace, for ten miles.

Some workout!

Yet for all her intense training, Jan remains relaxed and down-to-earth, approachable and candid in a very refreshing way.

The work *is* hard, but training for triathlon does have its bonuses: she can eat anything she wants—although Jan says she chooses her calories wisely, staying away from fats; her prize money pairs nicely with Steve's income as a pediatric dentist; and the acclaim is satisfying, too. The International Federation of Elite Triathletes ranked her number one in 1989 and she was selected the Triathlete of the Year. The IFET rankings are based and weighted on the quantity and quality of the competitive field in particular events. She also finished third in the 1989 Coke Grand Prix United States Triathlon Series.

And don't forget the opportunity to fly to places like the Caribbean and Europe. In 1989, only her third year of professional racing, Jan qualified for triathlon's first-ever World Championships in Avignon, France, and finished second behind New Zealand's Erin Baker. Both the U.S. men's and women's teams won gold medals, with the American women dominating Canada and West Germany. No wonder the Americans want triathlon to be an Olympic sport. Jan and daughter, Shelly, even got in a little sightseeing.

For Jan and Steve, that kind of personal involvement remains most important. Though both have received numerous Most Valuable Player awards, it's the role as Most Valuable Parent that they most cherish now. Steve and Jan nourish their family relationships by including their children wherever possible. For instance when Jan trains at LSU, she packs up her kids and half the neighborhood and takes them to the track. While Jan trains, the kids have fun playing in the pits near the high jump bar and long jump runway, along with chasing each other around the field. That schedule might not work for some families, but each member seems to have adjusted to the "ripples" in their family's lifestyle.

Jan's definitely not your average homemaker. She's made Opportunity her middle name. Although having children exacts a toll, she says she didn't just give up, saying, "I'm overweight, I'm flabby, I'll never be in shape . . .

"During the first delivery I can remember Steve saying the pain couldn't be any worse than a 200-meter butterfly. I looked over at him and said, 'This is *worse* than any 200-meter butterfly I *ever* swam!'" she laughs uproariously.

Each pregnancy meant adjusting to changes. After Shelly's birth Jan had a thyroid tumor removed. After Kyle's birth there was a hernia that had to be surgically repaired. And only eleven weeks after Kate's birth (in January 1984), Jan tried her first triathlon, a local event in Lexington, Kentucky, where Steve was doing his dental residency.

A newspaper account lauding a local female triathlete relit the former state swim champ's competitive desires and she thought she, too, could do that. Swimming and running came naturally and hadn't she known how to ride a bike since kindergarten? Plus, she comments, being a responsible young mother of three enhanced, not detracted from, her mental approach by teaching her discipline. Jan says she felt with the added maturity she could "just give it a try." Looking back, she says,

> I didn't really know how good I could be, or how much work it would take. When I started in triathlon we had no dreams or ideas that this is what I'd be doing *professionally*. Whenever someone brings it up, Steve credits me with supporting him through dental school and says how he wants to support me in this now. Maybe he felt a real conviction about that, but I never felt like I was doing anything but what I should be doing.
>
> There is no possible way that I could be doing triathlon without Steve. He is so supportive and so much a part of it, and he feels such a conviction that the Lord put me here. If he didn't feel that it would just be totally impossible. Steve and I both are confident that it's God's will because He's blessed it so mightily. I am sure if it were any

other way I would have reached my peak and I wouldn't have been able to continue.

Steve supports her in practical ways, not just wiggling his lips saying "attaway to go" but daily getting the kids up, dressed, fed, and their beds made before dropping them off at school. It frees Jan to do the major parts of her workout before the kids come home. "I meet my training partner and we swim at 6:30 in the morning. I mean, I'm practically through with one of my workouts before they are even in school. It's hard on us doing that every morning, but that's the only way we can manage.

"He does as much of the housekeeping as I do. He does whatever needs to be done and no one has a particular job. If he thinks the laundry needs to be done he is in there washing laundry or folding laundry—just whatever, he'll willingly do it."

The record-setting LSU Lady Tiger jokingly recalls that during her college years, when she qualified for three Association of Intercollegiate Athletics for Women swimming nationals, "if you kept competing past high school you were thought to be over the hill.

"And yet now, in this sport, triathlon, I am not even anywhere close to reaching my peak. Here I am one of the oldest in age, but one of the youngest in terms of experience. I have only been running seriously for three years, and running is the type of sport that just takes so much experience and time. I haven't reached my speed potential at all or the times that I can do for shorter distances. I am still not in the greatest condition that I can be in."

Almost unbelievably, she ended up winning that initial 1984 Lexington YMCA race despite the fact she was nursing baby Kate at that time. Shortly thereafter, she and Steve laid aside triathlon in preparing for a return to Baton Rouge to set up his pediatric dental practice. But only temporarily. Jan continued working out knowing that someday in the future there would be another race.

Jan grew up in an athletic Baton Rouge family, the fourth of six children of Robert J. and Mary Sue Meador. Bob, a three-sport letterman at LSU (basketball, baseball, and track) had been a basketball teammate of all-American and former pro Bob Pettit and current LSU athletic director Joe Dean, and had claimed a number of records, including one for consecutive starts which still stands.

Kentucky's Adolph Rupp had recruited Bob, a Louisville native, for basketball, but Bob chose LSU instead. After graduating, Bob pursued a baseball career and played outfield for the old Milwaukee

Braves before becoming a teacher, coach, and principal. Mary Sue also had been active at LSU, as a cheerleader and as a sorority member. Together, they instilled moral and spiritual values in their four sons and two daughters—along with a healthy dose of athletics. Jan remembers moving frequently when she was growing up. "I guess we kept outgrowing our home," she says of her family's frequent moves as the family kept adding kids.

Like father, like daughter, Jan excelled in various sports. But Bob's positive influence exceeded the athletic arena, affecting both Jan's self-image and her strong concept of God the father.

"Dad wanted us to dress like ladies and act like ladies in certain circumstances; but he also allowed us to be ourselves, whether it was playing basketball, running, swimming, or whatever. He was an athlete and he loved athletics and he wanted us to have that, too. It didn't matter that I was a girl, because I did every single thing my brothers did. But I feel fortunate that he also instilled that sense of pride through how I dressed and behaved," says Jan, one of the first female athletic scholarship winners at LSU. Jan followed her father's careful and loving guidance, although sometimes that meant giving up her own desires.

"I can remember wanting to try out for one particular sport but not being able to because he didn't approve of the personal lifestyle of the female coach. He tried to explain his reasoning to me even though he wasn't sure I'd understand, and I'm glad he did. He had a strong conviction that he didn't want me around those negative influences.

"Looking back, it kind of scared me to think that coach then might have started liking me in a wrong way," Jan comments. "And I realized later that while I was at LSU, there were probably women athletes who dated each other. I thought it was really strange. But you know, it goes on and each of us as women athletes are affected by that stigma to some extent," Jan says, referring to a common myth that a high percentage of female athletes are homosexuals.

While Jan accepted her parents' wisdom in moral matters, she already had her own firm spiritual foundation.

"I guess we were in church just about every time the doors opened. I didn't know anything else," she asserts. When she decided to accept Christ as her personal savior in the third grade, some around her doubted her commitment.

But looking back, I can tell you everything about that decision. I really understood that Jesus had died on the cross for my sin. I knew what I was doing, even though everyone else said I was too young.

My dad was such a big influence in my life, because I saw him living the Christian life and not just preaching about it. Actually, accepting Christ completely changed my life, even in the third grade, because so many of my later decisions were based on that one decision.

I remember asking Dad when I became a Christian how I'd know the difference between right and wrong. Like, how will I know the right thing to do? And my dad said, "Once you become a Christian you're filled with the Holy Spirit and He will show you right from wrong. You'll just have to trust Him." Jan's simple decision of faith grew as she matured both physically and spiritually.

"It was a healthy feeling, but it was almost like I was afraid to test God. I never went into a bar like many of my peers. And I can remember my friends telling me that I was innocent and naive and gullible. And they challenged my beliefs. But they were back-sliding and had to pay the price for their decisions. But they thought I was the dumb one to lead such a simple lifestyle. Because of that, at times I felt like an outcast, like I was a little bit different.

"I guess I never wanted to be in a bar or in any other compromising behavior when Jesus came back. I don't know what gave me those convictions, but I've always been that way."

Jan greatly respected her father, yet at times she chafed under his restrictions. "Looking back, though, I am really glad he was so strict. He wasn't hard on me and it wasn't that I felt pressure from him or was scared of him; it's just that my girlfriends had so much more freedom and, of course, I would have liked that. I had a curfew at 11:00.

"Then, when I'd graduated from college and moved back home before I got married, it was still only 11:30! I just accepted it. I didn't understand all his reasoning, but I didn't challenge it. And I didn't want to test God in the same way. To this day I love to please Dad."

Among other lessons Jan cites was Bob's emphasis that their athletic talents were God-given, like the God-given gifts of others, who had great voices or were smart in school. "He said you have to give the glory to God for the talent He's given you. And I can remember when I was in high school, whenever I was feeling like I had done something so great, God would let me know *He* was my strength.

"I still find that when I try to take credit for my accomplishments, I fall. I find it all the time," she says, and chuckles softly. "Found it last year when I had the number one ranking."

Jan relates how, after winning three of the first four 1989 U.S. Triathlon Series events and gaining the coveted top ranking, she had an opportunity at an awards banquet to thank God. "I can remember being afraid of thanking God publicly and so I didn't say anything like I usually do; not even a quick word of thanks." Money, competitive pride, and winning championships can lead to great personal self-satisfaction. And fear of being criticized or ostracized or being offensive causes hesitation.

"We are all different and we all have different witnesses," Jan says, departing briefly from her story. She adds that she prefers to share what Christ has meant to her in one-on-one conversations and through her life by standing up for Christ. "Others seem to be able to tell really big, huge crowds about their personal faith in God and go into it deeply, and to risk not being accepted."

Some of her triathlon peers see Christianity as "more of a religion than the relationship it really is," Jan believes. "People who are not Christians think you have these crazy beliefs and that it's a set of rules saying you can't do this and you can't do that, rather than the blessings and joys of faith in God. That's what they want to see because they don't want to accept Christ. They're looking to everything else for their meaning and purpose in life."

Jan continues evaluating that recent experience in her life:

> Perhaps I was kind of backsliding, not spending the time I usually do in prayer or Bible study. Maybe God wasn't my absolute number one priority.
>
> I had a selfish attitude of "I want to do this," and that meant I was living outside God's will. My priorities were wrong. It was almost like triathlon was controlling my life and I wasn't controlling it. Steve and I had always said that if that ever happened I would get out, especially if the family suffered. "We're out of it. We're through." But I can remember the kids being unbearable, and me being tired and overtrained—and yet thinking I was never doing enough. "Gotta do more, gotta do more. So-and-so's working harder than me. Gotta run more, gotta run more."

Jan says more and more hours were being devoted to the sport instead of to the family. "Then it was taken away just like that. I mean just like that," she says, snapping her fingers.

"Afterwards, I realized God was trying to bring me to my senses and make me more sensitive to Him. I don't know if it was Him shooting me down or *me* shooting me down! But either way it opened my eyes a lot and taught me a lot. And it brought our family closer together because I realized that a lot of times I would put my training and my races before my family. I came back so strong and with so much more faith."

The incident Jan refers to is when she was sidelined for a few months by a stress fracture in her left leg. As the injury healed, she reflected on her priorities, even while she did her running workouts by using a flotation device in a pool. "During that time, Steve wrote me a note that I still treasure. It says, 'Faith in the future gives us power over the present.' Faith in knowing that you are saved and that you have eternal life gives you power to get through every single day."

Jan started her competitive swimming career relatively late, at age thirteen. An LSU swimmer who coached a country club team saw their talent and recruited the young Meador kids. A month later Jan and younger brother Rick (a four-time NCAA all-American who now is head coach of the women's team at LSU) won three events each at a state meet. "We could only swim three days a week because the coaches couldn't get pool time, but we thought that was what everybody did. They didn't want us to know any better. They wanted us to think we had the same opportunities."

By age sixteen, improving swim times advanced Jan quickly into national rankings.

The summer of 1972 at a meet in Alexandria, Louisiana, she qualified for the Olympic Trials in the 100-meter butterfly. She says she was completely unaware of qualifying until informed by an interested coach who wanted to know if she was going to the Trials. "I said, 'What is that?' He just looked at me like I was crazy, and I said, 'You mean *the* Olympics?'"

Overwhelmed and excited, she sought out her dad and her own coach. The coach downplayed the opportunity because he knew that he was helpless to further train her, because the pool was available only a short time each day. "He couldn't really help us reach our potential because we were swimming such short yardages. But maybe because we really went so hard during that hour we were successful." Once again, increase the intensity with lack of duration.

Her parents made arrangements for Jan to train in Texas with a club team that had already qualified eight swimmers for the Olympic Trials. She could stay with the coach's family. Within days she was flying to Texas, but upon arrival her arms turned to butter and her Olympic hopes faded. Although just equalling a personal best would have gotten her into the finals, Jan was unused to the extraordinary increase in yardage and she swam slower at the Trials than her previous times.

"I went from an hour a day to three-and-a-half hours a day, five days a week. When I got to the Trials I was so exhausted I couldn't even get my arms out of the water." Awed by all the big-name swimmers, she went around collecting their snapshots for her photo album until she was stopped by her coach. "Lay that camera down," he growled. "You're here for the same reasons they are."

"But I didn't have that attitude. I didn't ever feel like I was there for the same reason they were. *They* were great swimmers." After that odyssey, Jan returned to Baton Rouge for her senior year of high school. It was fun being a cheerleader and playing basketball, she says. Still, away from the water, she felt uncomfortable showing her arms and her wide swimmer's shoulders.

"When I was the head cheerleader I used to always insist that we wear blouses under the sleeveless uniforms. I'd tell the girls it was supposed to be cold, and it would be 88 degrees! I was always ashamed of the way I was built because it wasn't accepted back in high school. Having muscles definitely was not in. It was considered masculine and unacceptable to have so much definition back in the seventies."

Casually dressed in denim jeans and a soft pink sweater with pinpoint lace collar, Jan appears energetic and physically fit, but no more so than a top-notch jazzerciser. However, when she's competing in her racing swimsuit, Jan's shoulders and biceps look unusually strong. Bodybuilders would envy her definition and muscle mass, for years of training are evident in her physique. Yet she doesn't train with weights because she has a tendency to build muscle mass, she says, which she doesn't need.

Steve helped me overcome that negative self-image because he would always tell me he loved broad shoulders and he loved an athletic look in a woman and that I should be proud of it. He made me start wearing sleeveless things and showing my arms, but I really had to overcome how I looked at myself. I always kind of felt that my sister, who was a beauty queen, had all the looks and that all the guys looked at her. But then I could see that in turn she wanted to be athletic like me.

Jan's high school swimming routine included frequent Saturday-morning workouts with the LSU men's swimming team, followed by breakfast at the athletic dorm. One particular Saturday she ran into some friends, football players who were supposed to be getting dates for some high school recruits. "Jan, you've got to do us a favor," they implored, begging her to go out with a certain linebacker from New Orleans. "We were supposed to get dates for them and we didn't, and we need to show those guys around campus," they told her.

"I said, 'Forget it. I am never going on a blind date.' They just begged me and begged me and I said, 'I can't do it.'"

Eventually Jan gave in protestingly after promises that her best friend would double date with another recruit. So she met Steve, who was also a swimmer and had competed the first couple of years of high school, and remembered Jan from some meets. She soon discovered that Steve had recently become a Christian at a youth retreat. Shortly after their blind date, Steve showed up at one of Jan's swim meets in New Orleans and met her family.

"Every couple of weekends he would come to Baton Rouge and we'd spend Saturday running around and visiting the local fast-food joints." They dated through college for five years. "It took him a year to give me a good-night kiss!" Jan exclaims.

"A lot of our friends in college didn't understand our relationship. Steve and I didn't feel like we had to see each other every night, but we knew couples that *had* to be together every minute. Steve was really into football and I was really into swimming and we accepted that in each other. These other couples would almost try to start us fighting and create jealousies, stuff like 'How do you know he is really studying?' From the very beginning we had such a trust in each other because we had a deep trust in the Lord. We were so busy that we didn't see each other all that much." Steve went on to be the starting linebacker, a captain, and the defensive Most Valuable Player.

"God just really put us together. We had so much in common," Jan recalls.

They kept their relationship fun, diving for golf balls on water hazards at golf courses, then cleaning the balls and selling them to pay for their movie dates. After both had graduated in 1977, they got married, and Jan worked as a swim coach while Steve went to dental school for four years. Afterwards Steve completed a residency program in Lexington for another two years. It was during that time in Kentucky, in 1980, 1982, and 1984, that Shelly, Kyle, and Kate were born. While living off Steve's meager stipend, with three children under four years of age, they had to be thrifty and resourceful. They managed to invest in a little house by borrowing some money from Steve's parents, but they resolved not to fall into the trap of using credit cards to buy temporary happiness.

Jan describes how her parents raised six children on a school principal's salary and her mom's secretarial pay. "I always wore hand-me-down clothing or else my grandmother made what I needed," she recalls, relating a story about being elected football homecoming queen during her senior year of high school. "Buying a dress then, like the other girls did, never entered my mind. I knew I wasn't going to. Like, 'Don't even ask because there's no money for it.' So we bought a pattern and asked Grandmother to make it."

Jan admits to becoming aware of being materialistic during the early years of marriage.

Before, there were always so many things I thought I needed, like a certain pair of shoes to go with a certain outfit. When you're single and working you can do those things, but when you're married and have three kids you're just trying to make ends meet. The money wasn't there; we couldn't overspend it, because we didn't have it. I had to overcome that materialistic attitude and learn to trust God with what He had given us.

But those days taught Steve and me so much and brought us so much closer together, when the pressure could have driven us apart.

Even now she greatly appreciates the lessons of learning to control their spending.

"Now, people say with our income we ought to increase our lifestyle. We've thought of buying a big house many, many times but neither one of us really wants it. We're perfectly satisfied where we are. Money has never been very important to me because I never had it before," she laughs.

Their first year in Lexington, their church Sunday school class hosted a formal Christmas progressive dinner. Most of the women were mothers who stayed at home, so dressing in party clothes was a special treat. For this one occasion, Jan greatly wanted a new outfit but knew they couldn't afford it.

While Steve was in school, Jan would push the kids up and

down the mall in the stroller because it was too cold to walk outside. She'd just window shop, never looking for anything in particular because she couldn't spend any money.

Coming home from one of those trips she spotted a woman's purse falling off the top of a car. Jan retrieved the purse, but couldn't catch up with the woman to return it. When Jan got home she opened the purse looking for a phone number. Inside she discovered over nine hundred dollars in cash and every major credit card, as well as the woman's phone number.

Jan telephoned persistently and finally reached the woman, who couldn't believe that her purse would be returned. "I said, 'Well of course I would call you. That's what anybody would do.'" The woman replied, astounded, "No, honey, that's not what anybody would do," and made arrangements to pick up her purse.

When they met, the woman pressed a hundred-dollar bill into Jan's hand—which Jan politely refused. But the woman persisted, "Otherwise I won't feel good about this, because you've not only returned my purse, you've saved me from having to contact all these credit card companies." Reluctantly, the younger woman finally accepted the reward. Jan recalls, "I took it and laughed about how good the Lord was to me. And Steve said, 'There's that dress and pair of shoes. God must have really thought you needed those!'

"Just that one experience taught me so much about being patient and trusting God to meet our needs. I got so many compliments on that new dress at the progressive dinner."

Jan fondly reminisces about another Christmas in Kentucky that was so frigid all the churches were closed on Sunday, Christmas Day that year. With the wind-chill factor at 30 degrees below, the little family of five nestled in front of the fireplace playing with the children's new toys and talking to one another, making future plans.

Yet it was not always this idyllic. The stress of being home with three preschoolers meant they were either going to have to replace the walls with rubber or buy a health club membership. One day Jan confessed to Steve that she had done the latter, and justified it by saying that she got a really good deal because there was a special in the paper. Steve knew Jan was bouncing off the walls so they took money from their savings to cover the expense. There was a free nursery at the club, but it had a one-hour time limit, so Jan worked out intensely. "Sorry I can't talk now," she recalls telling socializers, "because I have to get my babies from the nursery!" That hour was the best hour of the day, she says now.

Jan started triathlon competition again in 1986. After she'd won another race or two, she and Steve evaluated her possibilities. Sensing her potential, Jan dedicated herself to preparing to compete as a pro.

"Steve and I kept talking about it, wondering how I would do, and discussing a certain USTS race in Detroit. I had been racing only a year and I knew all the top women, including Kirsten Hanssen, were going to be there, and that it would be a good test of my abilities."

They decided on three USTS events that year and in Detroit she hesitantly introduced herself to Kirsten (then the top-ranked female triathlete) and wished her a good race. "I'm kind of new. I wanted to meet you. My name is Jan. I am a Christian, and I heard you are, too," Jan recalls saying. Kirsten won that event while Jan finished fifth. They soon became fast friends. Jan was even a bridesmaid in Kirsten's November 1989 wedding to Robert Ames.

Jan competed full-time in 1987 and in 1989 raced in eighteen events. Generally she leaves on Friday and returns on Sunday evening after a race. But she trained on Saint Croix for two and a half weeks prior to the America's Paradise Triathlon in April, 1989, where she finished third.

She has gone through various bikes, making mistakes yet learning constantly, picking up pointers. Now, she's nearly unbeatable in her favorite leg of the triathlon. Her bike sponsor is Light Speed, and she's part of the Pioneer Electronics racing team of five men and five women, including world champion Mike Pigg.

"I'm not away from the children as much as if I had an 8:00-to-5:00 job. Usually I'm done by the time they're home," Jan says. But at first, she says, she wasn't sure whether her children understood or appreciated her efforts. "Sometimes when you're frustrated and down, and you've just had a hard workout or you've just had a hard day, you wonder how much more you can take. And then only an hour later you've renewed your mind and you find yourself talking all about training and competition."

One such day, a discouraged Jan hadn't gotten in all her workout and mentioned it to oldest daughter Shelly. "I told her, 'Maybe Mom should just retire. I didn't even get my run in and I'm turning complacent.' And she told me not to do that. When I asked her why not, she said, 'I love you being a triathlete. Plus everybody knows me because of you.' I said, 'Shelly, now that's not right.' She said, 'Well, you know. They know me because of me, too. But it's kind of nice, because everybody at school knows my mom.' So she's really proud. I mean *really* proud. She even had her whole school praying for me when I had the stress fracture."

Jan says she's often asked in interviews why she goes through such bodily punishment. At her first Hawaii Ironman Triathlon (1987), she ended up crawling across the finish line and staying overnight in the hospital. Fearful of becoming dehydrated going through the black lava fields in her first marathon, she actually had imbibed too much fluid and gained twelve pounds. Because of the resulting electrolyte imbalance, she became disoriented. The next year reporters inquired why she was back. Didn't she remember the pain? Hadn't she already put her body to the ultimate test?

> I told them the only thing I could possibly compare it to is having babies; you hurt so bad and then you hold that little baby in your arms and totally forget about the pain you just went through. You have this little miracle in your arms.
>
> That's sort of like racing. You hurt so bad when you cross the finish line, but you can also have such a good feeling because you challenged yourself and you met the challenge. You can't remember the pain—until you get into the next 10k!
>
> Sometimes in a race when you have that same awful hurt and pain, you cry out to the Lord saying you can't go on. And then you feel God's strength just pouring into you. At those times I can visualize the Cross and Jesus' suffering and I can focus on that. There is no way I am ever going to hurt that bad, no matter what I do to my body. I am never going to feel that type of suffering like when Jesus took all our sin on Himself and paid the price.
>
> I think when I focus on other people's pain or compare it to Christ's pain, my own problems seem so small.

Jan recounts a visualization technique she learned from LSU basketball coach Dale Brown that she now uses in running longer distance races. For each mile she thinks of a person and their pain and suffering and focuses on that. From mile one to mile two, it's one person. From mile two to mile three, it's another. Until the last mile.

> I always have Jesus Christ on that last mile. When reporters ask me why I compete and put my body through such things, I can honestly say it's because I realize Jesus carried me. He carried the Cross and the persecution and the shame for me. He went through that. This is my last mile and it's not nearly as bad as what He did to carry that Cross.
>
> Lately I've been wondering how in the world non-Christians can

put their bodies through what we do. I don't know. I don't know how they can put their bodies through that pain threshold without Jesus' help. I can't do any more than what I'm doing. And I couldn't do it without His strength.

Training for the Ironman necessitates up to six hours a day on the bike. That cycling is all done on the Great River Road, a straight, uninterrupted stretch of pavement along the Mississippi River, running to New Orleans. It's so picturesque, it seems Jan could really get into the flow just like that mighty river. Except it's below the levee, and the only change of scenery daily is where the cows have ambled into the pastures.

Jan feels it's good discipline to pedal those lengthy bike rides in the Baton Rouge humidity and she goes back and forth with Kirsten regarding which is the better training site. Kirsten trains in the Colorado altitude with no humidity, but Jan thinks she gets the advantage of the toughest environment. "Confidencewise, we each think we're in the best environment and that's the whole ball game there, mental confidence."

Jan had a great season in 1989, adding to her runner-up finish at the world championships a second-place showing at the U.S. Nationals at Hilton Head, South Carolina, in early November and a victory in the National Sprint Championships in Miami a few weeks later. At Hilton Head, she led until the last 300 meters when Joy Hansen caught up and beat her by a mere eight seconds. After that she vowed of the short-course nationals, "They'll never catch me in the run. It's only three miles!" and won an event that also included an 800-meter swim and a 15-mile bike ride.

Jan's future plans include triathlon events in 1990, plus joining a cycling team while preparing to make a transition to cycling road events in 1991. Then in 1992, she'll concentrate on making the U.S. Olympic team in cycling. Jan, who insiders say is the strongest cyclist in women's triathlon, feels her chances are good for achieving that goal, nearly twenty years after her first Olympic attempt, in swimming.

"Those are my goals and this is what Steve and I have purposed to do, but I'm realistic in that we don't know whether we'll even be here tomorrow. That's the way I look at it. I just take it one day at a time," she says.

After that, Jan mentions retiring from so much traveling and focusing on the Tour de France. After that, who knows? Perhaps the Tour de Ripple with Steve and the kids!

# 16

## "Cindy"

### Entering His courts
### with praise

This chapter is a true story about how one female athlete has battled homosexuality. However, because of the sensitive nature of this subject, names and locations have been changed to protect the privacy of the individuals involved. "Cindy" is so committed to helping others avoid the kind of difficulties she's been through that she would gladly reveal her identity. But to protect the identity of others, she must remain anonymous.

The issue of homosexuality in women's athletics is one which can remain silenced no longer. Whether through innuendo or direct accusation, women athletes and coaches are encompassed by this issue. I believe the Bible states clearly in Romans 1:24–32 that God condemns homosexual behavior.

Yet there is hope.

Through the shed blood of Jesus Christ, there is forgiveness.

In 1 Corinthians 6:9–10, Paul speaks against various lifestyle behaviors including homosexuality. Then he adds, "And such were some of you; but you were washed, but you were sanctified, but you were justified in the name of the Lord Jesus Christ, and in the Spirit of our God" (v. 11). In 1 John 1:9 we see that Jesus willingly forgives our transgressions when we ask. We become sanctified (set apart) and justified (just as if we'd never sinned) through Jesus.

It's with great respect that I commend Cindy for her courage and her forthrightness in addressing such unhealthy relationships and for sharing how God has helped her deal with her difficulties. But I realize that perhaps some parents, after reading this story, might be inclined to dissuade their daughters from participating in sports. I *contend that it's not the athletic participation, but the individual's feminine self-image that needs examination.*

*I encourage godly parents and teachers and other influencers of young people to look beyond the distastefulness of the topic and recognize the father's important role in influencing his daughter's self-esteem. According to Christian coaches of female athletes, many times these young ladies have a greater fear of failing to be a feminine woman than of failing on the athletic field. Now, here's Cindy's story.*

CHRISTMAS DAY, A DAY TO CELEBRATE the miracle birth of that infant Jesus so many years ago. A time children unleash that excitement pent-up with each added package under the tree. A moment for memories.

It was no different in 1969 for nine-year-old Cindy. Sure, she lived in an inner-city tenement, a wasteland of emotion in a desert of hope. For ghetto-bound individuals, Help Wanted signs become symbols of opportunities wasted. There's a daily reminder on the streets that you just don't measure up. And the dark of night brings its own grim reminders.

Each night a family member, one of twelve living in the three-bedroom flat, served on rat-patrol duty, alertly banging on the ceiling and walls to dissuade the marching army of rats. It was better they invade another family's quarters. As an infant Cindy had to contend not with furry teddy bears and baby bunnies in her crib, but with fuzzy rats, real live ones.

Even so, Christmas still comes to brighten the ghetto, if only for a few hours. And that particular morning young Cindy delightedly discovered a beautiful, shiny bicycle for herself and one for her older brother Marc. It was an answer to her dreams! But sometimes dreams become nightmares. Unfortunately, that's true too frequently in the inner city and Cindy's time for joy would become a time for tears.

"As a kid growing up in the city, all I ever really wanted was a bike," says Cindy, now a teacher in her thirties. When she was six, she had carefully saved her coins in a piggy bank to buy a bike, only to have a family member break it while she was at school, stealing her money for a heroin fix. Small change can be pretty big to an addict. Cindy had valued that piggy bank because it was the only thing of value she owned, definitely a prized possession. Young Cindy had been devastated, but what could she do? She had been left with nothing except the painful memory. But now, getting a bicycle on Christmas day, that was great!

Off she set on her new bike, wind in her face, legs pumping excitedly. The little girl headed for a nearby high school, perhaps protected from cars, but unshielded from potential thugs. Tragedy struck once again.

"That Christmas day, three teenage boys came up and told me to get off that bike, and stole it from me that very moment," she recalls. Not once, but twice was she burned in pursuing her dream of a bike. Her Wheels of Fortune were Wheels of Misfortune. Her Ticket to Ride was stalled at the station. Moreover, there were other, even more difficult things to contend with.

One was not knowing her birth father, who was Italian. Cindy's mother was black and she wanted to have two children and raise them to be "Hollywood stars." Her dream for Cindy was that she be a prima ballerina or an actress, a queen on the silver screen—definitely on-stage somewhere. Cindy, however, would become a basketball star, a queen shooting behind a screen, not performing on one.

"I never saw a picture of my birth father. He's just a name they have on my birth certificate," says Cindy. "As a youngster, I couldn't understand the lasting effects of not knowing who my real father was. I suppose it was the same thing that most people who've been adopted eventually come to grips with—the desire to know that person who was their parent and to see that person."

Cindy not only had a childlike curiosity about "Who am I?" and "Where do I come from?" but a deeper need for a sense of identity and belonging. She did not look like her mother's side of the family. "And since there was no father's side of the family, the only family I ever had was my mom's side with my grandparents and Mom's brothers and sister, but I didn't feel like I looked like any of them. I didn't have that sense of belonging."

Those uncertainties were compounded by a lack of affection in her nuclear family. They didn't hug or express emotion, or tell each other that they loved them, creating an emotional deficit in Cindy. When the family moved during her freshman year to an exclusively white community, not only did Cindy feel like she didn't fit in at home, she didn't feel like she fit in at her new school either. And there were added adjustments to make in the preteen's fragile self-identity.

"I was never asked to the prom or slumber parties. There weren't many friends, real friends, and certainly not boyfriends, because in that community I was rejected because of my race, because of being only half white," Cindy recalls.

A striking beauty, the 5-foot-8-inch Cindy tried to find areas where she would be accepted, where talents might earn her respect and friends and attention. She worked hard to earn the A's of acceptance, attention, and affection through academics and athletics. But a foundation like that is fragile at best, determined by performance and always hanging on the last accomplishment. Who you are can only be determined by acknowledging Jesus Christ as your Lord and Savior and allowing Him to fill the voids and uncertainties, not by trying to perform for an ever-critical audience that demands increasingly more.

Her grandmother's penchant for providing Cindy with educational games as a youth paid off academically and she excelled in her high school courses. Grades came naturally and Cindy exhibited a real gift for learning.

In athletics, she worked diligently and eventually her talent would pay off with travel on basketball teams going to the Far East, Europe, the Soviet Union, and Poland, as well as earn her a college scholarship to a prestigious university, and a brief pro career. The basketball court was her stage, and she played the game with a passion.

"I enjoyed basketball tremendously, and I loved to play all the time. I was the high school standout and people wanted to know me, but more because of what I could do than who I was. That's where I gained my acceptance," she recalls. If performance was a yardstick of Cindy's acceptance, then impressive performances won her myriad friendships during her high school years.

As a sixteen-year-old, she attended the Eastern region women's Olympic basketball tryouts. Never before had women's basketball been included in the Olympics and just making the team would be historic. One hundred forty-six hopefuls assembled in Connecticut on a hot May weekend and only five would qualify for the national camp. Although she was the youngest competing, the high school sophomore assessed her competition with a street-wise confidence born in the ghetto.

"To my surprise, the people trying out had been my counselors at a basketball camp I'd attended. I thought for sure I could compete with them, since we had played all the time at the camp," she says, intimating that she had out-performed them. The players were mostly college stars and recent graduates, even a young coach or two. As Cindy had brashly predicted, she survived each cut, making the twenty invited back for the final scrimmages on Sunday.

In games of one-on-one and three-on-three, the sophomore's city playground skills attracted attention. In half-court games, she paired up with a record-setting collegiate scorer and a future Olympian. The trio was crushing all comers until the whistle blew signaling the tryout's end. Spent, having given everything, Cindy awaited the proclamation of the five finalists who would be invited to the national Olypmic tryout camp. But instead, in a surprise move, the coaches announced a full-court scrimmage.

"I started getting a little cocky. I had given everything and I was exhausted. When we had to go full-court, fifteen minutes straight of international rules, I dribbled off my foot and threw the ball away. The coach said later she wanted to see who could play best under fatigue. So, I didn't make that cut."

Cindy learned from that experience not only how to handle stress and fatigue, but also that she had some talent with a potential future involving international travel. After that performance prior to her junior year, Cindy was named a preseason all-American by every basketball ranking from *Parade Magazine* to the Converse and Adidas all-star teams. She got the opportunity to try out for the U.S. Women's Select Team representing the United States at a competition in Asia. Making that team as a high school junior was an honor, but by traveling and being with older women, she would have her eyes opened to more than a simple cross-cultural experience.

Young and impressionable, she was approached and seduced by a female athletic trainer. Today, she describes that experience.

As a seventeen-year-old girl who had not experienced any kind of romantic involvements or relationships or even an affectionate family, I was a starving person in terms of affection. I hadn't really even kissed anyone before in my life. I had had zero displays of affection.

"Emily" showed me a great deal of affection and then, I hesitate to say it because I wish it wasn't true, she took advantage of me. And I say that rather than "abused," because I was such a willing recipient. After all I'd been through in my life, I desperately wanted someone to love me, and unfortunately I equated real love with physical love. It was also the first time I'd been away from home. I was very naive and totally unprepared for what happened.

That was my first exposure to a same sex relationship or anything like homosexuality. I had no clue what was happening or how it would affect my life later. And I share this in order to help others see how such incidents have deeper, long-term consequences. These things have happened to me, but I know God can turn them to His good.

I knew physically what was happening, but I really didn't know emotionally what was happening, except that here was a person who was showing me the kind of affection that I had always craved and never received. And it felt good to be wanted or to feel like somebody cared about me in a loving way. But in retrospect, I wish she had never come into my life.

Cindy's confusion was accentuated by other traumatic events which had occurred earlier.

From the ages of eleven to fourteen, Cindy had been molested by a close male acquaintance. "I thank God there was no intercourse with him," she says, "but there was a lot of fondling and molestation, and that too is a violation, an abuse. Those are very formative years, especially in terms of understanding who you are as a sexual being. Because I had been abused and violated as a youngster, that proper foundation of sexual identity was destroyed. Then when I got involved with Emily there was more destruction to that foundation."

In Cindy's senior season, again the on-court accolades mounted. She set a state single-game scoring record. She was recruited by nearly every major college and accepted a scholarship to play at a Division I school with an excellent academic reputation. And before her freshman college year began, she made the inaugural Olympic Sports Festival. While Cindy was competing there she met a man who encouraged her to attend the Fellowship of Christian Athletes meetings at her college.

The next year Cindy began going to the meetings, but mostly to meet people, because doing so always made her feel better about herself. Cindy met more than a few new friends, she met a Friend who would help her to feel accepted, the Lord Jesus Christ. She was impressed by the genuine love the group of athletes had for each other and the joy in their lives. This construction crew of committed Christians began building positive things into her life through their discipleship, fellowship, Bible study, and witness.

"They explained that I couldn't serve both God and man; that I would cling to one and despise the other. God wanted to be number one, and basketball could still be there, but He wanted that top position. I had to decide what was most important. I had always had a reverence for God as a child, but no formal religious training. I didn't know what it meant to be a Christian. I didn't know how to express that reverence, and basketball was what I was dedicated to."

So, after careful consideration, Cindy prayed with one of her new friends and invited Jesus Christ into her life. She embraced her new faith with a fervency previously unequalled over anything else in her life, including basketball. Because of her desire to know Christ in a deeper way and get involved in her faith, she decided to forego her junior year, red-shirting, meaning in her case, not only could she not play in games but neither could she practice with the team. Teammates were bewildered by the "new" Cindy. The coach was stunned and lashed out critically in the newspapers, her pride hurt that Cindy had seemingly rejected her sincere and well-meant attempts to mold Cindy's troubled self-esteem. Cindy was grateful for her coach's help, but self-sufficiency was not what she needed. Christ-sufficiency was the answer.

"My coach was hurt that I had found Christ on my own, rejecting the self-help measures she had tried to instill. But 'success' is not what's going to last. What God gives us is so much greater. The new friendships I established in the Christian world [and apart from the basketball team] were so much better lasting and genuine. That is a trade I would make again and again and again. God honored tremendously that commitment to spend a year learning more about Jesus." When Cindy regained her eligibility, she exhibited a peace and joy that overcame any potential friction with the team and she regained her basketball prominence.

"God really restored my relationship with my coach. In fact, she gave me the nickname 'the politician' because I was always kissing babies and introducing myself, and it always looked like I was on the campaign trail. She and I enjoyed a real friendly relationship, especially my senior year."

After graduation, Cindy worked for a year before being drafted by a team in a new women's pro basketball league. A modest salary met her needs, but better yet, Cindy used her platform as a professional athlete to proclaim her faith in Christ and organize chapel services prior to games. Then the league folded and Cindy was invited by a friend to move out West. There, she thought, her troubled past could remain hidden so that she could freely develop her personal walk with the Lord. She found a church home soon after arriving.

"One day my pastor had a sermon on 'the father heart of God,' about the earthly father's role as nurturer and what you're supposed to receive from your parents." Deep turmoil surfaced where before it had been hidden. Cindy was unaware of the source of her anguish until then. Years of pain erupted, unable to be held back.

Cindy came face to face with her past—the anguish over not knowing her real father, the humiliation of earlier sexual abuse, the anguish of being victimized by the older lesbian athletic trainer. She broke down, crying out to God when she got home, distraught that such pain had entered her life.

> I shared it with my roommate, and I was crying. I don't typically cry, because I'm not very emotional. That's a characteristic of being a victim, like I was. I've been getting counseling now through a pastor and have read a book that's helped me deal with my past. It's called *Pain and Pretending,* by Rich Bueler.

> But that night I cried like I've never cried before or since. I cried for hours until there were no tears left. I fought, because I was experiencing the hurt of an eleven-year-old who had been violated. And I had to cry out the hurt from years of abuse.

> And I also experienced anger about the earlier abuse and what that man did to me, for the hurt he caused and for the consequences of that hurt—the lack of affection and my craving for it in the wrong places, in a same-sex relationship because it was convenient.

> God was telling me to forgive that man, and my roommate was telling me to forgive him, and it was an incredibly emotional night. I eventually came to the point where I could speak that forgiveness and really mean it.

> As I've come to understand God's forgiveness through Jesus Christ's sacrifice on the Cross, I have been restored in my relationship to Him. I so desire to have a family. I want to get married and have kids.

Indeed, knowing that desire, friends are always trying to fix her up with eligible young men.

As she is trusting God with her past, her background has given her a valuable perspective on what good friendships entail. Cindy comments on that.

"I think most homosexual relationships are ones of convenience, at least the ones I've seen. We all desire intimacy. It's convenient to develop friendships with teammates—we play on the same team, go to the same school—and we spend so much time together that we share emotional things that have happened and become emotionally dependent. Emotional dependency often leads to physical expression, and that sometimes leads to a physical relationship.

"It's convenient and that's the hard thing to break off. If there aren't good role models to show that you don't need to get your nurturing from that type of relationship and that you don't need to pursue intimacy on that level, then it's going to continue to be a problem in women's athletics because we spend so much time together as athletes. That's why a book like this is long overdue, so that young women have a group of role models to look up to. For me, because of what I've been through, it's so important to be able to express that there's hope through Jesus in overcoming all our hurt and disappointment."

Cindy seeks the guidance of her assistant pastor and his wife and feels accountable to them, as though she's become a part of their family. But because her work schedule is so heavy, there's little time for building relationships. "Being a Christian single woman is very difficult," she says. "It limits the field because I want the men I date to be strong believing Christians." But while she waits for the Lord to fulfill her desire for marriage and family, she carries the hope and conviction that God is in control of her life and that she's not locked into a lifestyle of destruction.

"I have no doubt that my relationship with the man who encouraged me to attend the Fellowship of Christian Athletes when I started college kept me from going into the gay lifestyle wholeheartedly. I really thank God for bringing this special man into my life.

"Because of my growth in Christ, I feel better about being able to say no in various areas of my life," she says. "A person who's struggled with the incidents I have struggled with would want to meet other people's every need. I just don't want to be so busy that I forget about my first priority and that's my relationship with the Lord. I don't want others to dictate to me in regard to my time, my emotions, or my body. I know that I'll be more cautious in my friendships.

"I feel that now I've renewed my commitment to pursuing God and to be devoted to that covenant I've established with Him. There's a story in the Bible that really describes how I feel: Luke 7:36–50. Jesus says basically he who is forgiven much, loves much; and he who has been forgiven little, loves little. I know that forgiveness He offers and only desire to share my experiences as a reminder of that.

"God knows the desires of my heart, and I think as I allow Him to heal those wounds and renew my life, that those desires for marriage and children will be fulfilled. I pray they will."

Author's note: After this chapter was written, Cindy became engaged to be married.

RIGHT: Two-Time Ms. Olympia, Bodybuilder Rachel McLish (photo by Harry Langdon)
BELOW: 1989 Triathlete of the Year Jan Ripple, husband Steve, and children (from left) Kate, Kyle, and Shelly